Follow Your Bliss

Hal Zina Bennett, Ph.D.,
& Susan J. Sparrow

AN AUTHORS GUILD BACKINPRINT.COM EDITION

Follow Your Bliss

Discovering Your Inner Calling and Right Livelihood

All Rights Reserved © 1990, 2004 by Hal Zina Bennett & Susan Sparrow

AN AUTHORS GUILD BACKINPRINT.COM EDITION

Published by iUniverse, Inc.

For information address:

iUniverse, Inc.

2021 Pine Lake Road, Suite 100

Lincoln, NE 68512

www.iuniverse.com

Originally published by Avon Books

The author extends his gratitude for permission to publish excerpts from *An Open Life* by Joseph Campbell and Michael Toms. Copyright © 1988 by New Dimensions Foundation. Reprinted by permission of Harper & Row, Publishers, Inc.

ISBN: 0-595-31659-X

Printed in the United States of America

Dedicated to our children,
Who have taught us to see
Brief, sparkling glimpses
Of truth and love beyond
The illusions of our wisdom.

Acknowledgments

As anyone who has done much teaching knows, our greatest lessons often come through our students. This has surely been true for both of us. Over our lifetimes we have been blessed with friends, students, business associates, clients, and coworkers who have generously shared their lives with us. To all we are deeply indebted, and although it would be impossible to list each of you by name, we would hope that when you read these words you might know who you are and feel, for a moment, our gratitude. Thank you all, once again, for sharing your struggles, your successes, and wisdom with us.

Contents

INTRODUCTION

Traveling to the Inner World

I feel that if one follows what I call one's bliss—the thing that really gets you deep in the gut and that you feel is your life—doors will open up. They do!
> —Joseph Campbell, *An Open Life: Joseph Campbell in Conversation with Michael Toms*

Over the past few years, we conducted a series of exploratory workshops on learning to trust your own inner guidance. Most participants were in their early thirties and forties, the so-called "Baby Boomers," now seeking to satisfy inner needs that they had not been able to satisfy through acquiring more money, status, or expensive toys. Their quests for greater meaning in their lives had led them back to themselves. They were seeking to satisfy what sometimes seemed very elusive inner promptings. And many were finding that they could satisfy these needs only through creative efforts, useful public service, and in the development of more loving connections with other people, the environment, and themselves.

They found themselves looking for jobs and avocations

where their lives could make a real difference. Although the choices varied widely, many people gravitated toward activities such as world peace, international cooperation, improving the environment, health, love, human compassion, and harmony. Listening to these people's stories, we had to consider the very real possibility that, in all of us, our inner guidance encourages us to reach beyond the boundaries of our physical existence and to touch our spiritual essence.

In our workshops, we have learned what a powerful force the inner self really is for all of us. We can suppress it, simply not be aware of it for periods of time, or even have it crushed early in life, but we can never get rid of it. Sometimes it is like a tiny voice in the wilderness; at other times it is loud, clear, and direct. When we learn to stop, listen, and follow the guidance that it provides, we experience bliss, or at the very least, a deep sense of personal fulfillment. When we don't stop to listen, for one reason or another, we experience frustration and a sense that our lives are empty. .

One workshop we offered was called "Healing the Adult Wounded Child." We had originally intended this for people who had suffered rather severe wounds as children, people who as adults still carried the secret hurts of an unfortunate childhood. These people, we had discovered, found it unusually difficult to develop a strong sense of their own inner guidance or to believe in their own personal strengths and self-worth.

A large percentage of the people who came to these workshops were children of alcoholics, while some had been the victims of rape, incest, and emotional abuse. As they shared their life stories with us, it was always easy to understand why their struggles for self-knowledge and trust in their own inner guidance were so difficult. They resisted going into their inner worlds because to do so was to relive the awful pain of their youngest years, pain that they wanted to put behind them.

What at first surprised us was that many people who had had what seemed, by contrast, to have been rather ordinary childhoods, with loving, well-meaning parents, also signed up for these workshops. When they shared their stories, the descriptions of the wounds seemed pale next to those whose childhoods were marred by rather severe physical or emotional abuse. But then an interesting thing occurred: We all found ourselves as deeply moved by these people's stories as by those with more dramatic tales to tell. We soon came to realize that beneath the surface, there were common themes that gave us all a common bond. The wound that undermined trust in our own inner guidance, making bliss more and more inaccessible, had little to do with the manner in which the wound was inflicted. As someone once said during a workshop: "The wound can be inflicted with a sledgehammer or a feather, but can cause as much damage either way."

During a workshop we were giving one evening, a participant who described himself as an "armchair sociologist" quoted some interesting figures to us. He said that according to a number of leading psychologists and sociologists (Virginia Satir, Eric Erikson, and others), at least 70 percent of us come from "dysfunctional" families. This means that we were raised in families where alcoholism, drug abuse, battering, and emotional violence—or other subtler but no less emotionally crippling dynamics—were prevalent. The result is that millions of us distrust our inner worlds, yet long to feel "connected and whole." To feel connected and whole, we must, of course, draw closer to our inner worlds; but our backgrounds have taught us to push away from them, to avoid the memories of pain and confusion that we harbor within.

As we each shared stories and loving support in the workshops, it became clear that regardless of the nature of the wound, most people suffered from feelings of being detached, alone, distrustful of their own views of reality, bewildered by their own choices, and often severely alienated from life. And the *healing*, when it came, was always the same: getting in touch with our own inner guidance, and finally experiencing it as profoundly comforting, coming from a source much greater than ourselves.

When we open inward and learn what it is to follow our bliss, we pass through an imaginary gateway and enter the reality of our inner worlds to discover our own personal resources. We identify and automatically begin dissolving self-imposed limitations. The self-knowledge we gain by opening inward can be profound and gratifying, erasing old grievances and releasing us from guilts and anxieties that had always seemed to be "just part of everyday living." Above all, opening inward puts us in touch with our own inner guidance. Our belief is that as we do this, we can all learn to better understand the messages that come to us through our own consciousnesses, our own hearts, our own psyches, our own bodies, and our own spirits.

From the people who participated in our workshops, we learned much. And what became clearer and clearer as we went along was that we were all ultimately happier, more productive, more able to receive and express love, when we got in touch with our own inner guidance and gained the courage to follow it.

The workshops and consulting naturally led to our plans to write this book. When we started writing it, we were not at all sure what to call it. Titles for books, like names for one's children, are not to be taken lightly. Although "Opening Inward" hinted at some of the themes we wished to cover, it really wasn't focused enough. It didn't convey the message that we felt was the key.

Then we heard Michael Toms's interviews with Joseph Campbell on "New Dimensions Radio," and later on, watched the very popular public television interviews that Bill Moyers taped with the same author. The tremendous popularity of both these series encouraged us, confirming what we had observed in the workshops we had been teaching.

Joseph Campbell had been an important influence in our own lives during our college days in the 1960s, when his book *The Hero with a Thousand Faces* was required reading in so many literature classes. It seemed to us that he had a message then that a whole generation, ourselves included, was only now coming around to fully appreciate.

In the Toms and Moyers interviews, Campbell spoke of his years as a teacher at Sarah Lawrence College. When young people came to him, asking for his advice about what they should do with their lives, his recommendation was always the same: "Follow your bliss," he would tell them. When we heard this phrase, we knew we had the title for our book. It was not only that the title fit, it was that we had once again been reminded of our debt to Campbell. And so there would be for us a sense of completion in paying homage to a man whose writings had opened so many doors for us.

LESSONS FROM THE 1960S

Although it is as old as humanity itself, for us the theme of following our bliss had its roots in the sixties. Many dreams, which so many of us shared in our early adult years, continue to inspire us in ways that perhaps very few previous generations have known. For whatever else we might question from our youth, there are certain themes that continue to capture our attention because they strike upon human needs and human possibilities that none of us can ignore. There are certain key themes of the sixties that epitomize our own convictions, or at least our instincts, that there is something essential and true about following one's own inner guidance and living a life where one's creative and spiritual potentials are recognized. We would prefer this to blindly following a well-worn path that society has laid out for us. And, in a very real way, that is what this book is about.

What was important about the sixties? If it was nothing

else, it was a time to look inward, a time to discover our own creative and spiritual gifts. And it was also a time to push the limits, to risk it all and challenge every convention, from sexuality to spirituality and everything in between. It was a time to discover individual possibilities, both the positive and the negative, and to learn how this knowledge could improve the quality of life on our planet.

It was a time to discover our own human gifts and to learn the power of sharing those gifts with others. And a time to discover that love was something more than a private sentiment that we must reserve exclusively for our own families.

For a while, back in the sixties, we were relatively free of social and economic restraints, and the social movement we shared was large enough to let us feel that we had widespread support in our beliefs, that we were on the right track even though we were—at least on the surface—defying tradition. Years later we began to see that the dream had its downside. There were casualties, some of them tragic, some comic, ranging from broken hearts to broken minds to disillusionment, and from economic disaster to spiritual bewilderment, and more. Everyone who shared the dream also shared these losses and heartaches. Then the sudden economic crunch of the seventies made the easy life of the sixties, with low rents and free medical clinics and cheap transportation, and sometimes even free food, a thing of the past. It was time to step back and take another look at our lives.

If we ever hoped to reap something enduring from the experiment we'd been living, we were going to have to figure out how to build bridges from the perhaps overconfident experiments of our utopian subculture back into mainstream society. How were we going to make use of beliefs that had been created by the synergy of a whole generation or two of dreamers, rebels, madmen and madwomen, saints, visionaries, and geniuses? How were we ever going to sort out the purely fanciful, and maybe even insane, from what was truly useful, creative, productive, and beneficial to humankind as a whole? The task, as we moved into middle age, was one of seeking ways to use what we had learned from the sixties to build a foundation that would serve us in our own later years and would continue to serve our own children and the generations that would follow them.

A SPIRITUAL RENAISSANCE

Today we are living in a spiritual renaissance that perhaps is like no other in history. One of the things that makes it unique is that the search for spiritual values is not associated with any institution and does not depend on traditional religious terms or symbols. Rather we see these spiritual concerns guided by the heart.

We see our new spiritual concerns expressed in a renewed interest in harmonious personal relationships, and in once again embracing the family, and in finding healthful camaraderie with our neighbors and coworkers. It is being discovered and expressed in the miraculous healing power of love being brought into modern medicine, and in opening communications that have too long been closed with the people of other countries. It is found in our seeking a world without war, and in seeking ways to heal our own planet from the environmental wounds we have inflicted on her, so that we may once again live in accord with nature.

Words such as "spiritual" and "love" are no longer seen as mere sentiments. Rather, they are seen as ways of referring to certain qualities of life and our relationships with one another, our planet, and with a Higher Power which is the source of all life. These words are seen even in the results-oriented environment of the business community, where not so long ago only the language of productivity and the marketplace was considered acceptable.

At the center of this renaissance is a vision of each individual as an important expression of a spiritual "whole" that is much greater than any one of us can even imagine. In the Old Testament, we are told that "Mankind is One," and this principle is carried forward into our new spiritualism.

Throughout the pages ahead, we will be discussing how inner guidance connects us all with a loving, universal consciousness that is much larger than ourselves. We will explore how each of us is an important part of a universal consciousness and how we each have within us a kind of homing device that directs our lives so that we can fulfill our roles in the larger universal plan intended for us.

We have a choice between blocking inner guidance and following paths that actually take us further and further from our life purpose, and learning to apply the signals of inner guidance so that we might enjoy the deep satisfaction of living our lives to the fullest, following the path of the loving universal force that is our Creator and ultimate Guide.

As we were writing this book, we realized that there were certain beliefs which we share as authors and as partners in life, beliefs which form the core of the work we present here. The primary one that applies to following one's bliss is our conviction that each one of us has a unique life purpose, a gift that unfolds and is revealed to us through our vocations, our relationships with other people, and in our responses to the challenges and joys of daily life. We believe that this life purpose is a gift that we received, perhaps at our conception, and that we brought into the world at our births.

Along with the gift, we inherit a responsibility for bringing all that we are into the world, thus returning the power of the gift in its mature form. We do this by following our bliss, by learning to read the messages of ease, pleasure, and self-satisfaction that accompany those moments when we are on our true paths. We believe that each one of us experiences the presence of this responsibility within us. We feel it as the drive for self-expression, self-realization, and the will to share our deepest thoughts and feelings with others.

Through the larger consciousness, of which we are an expression, we have been given the gift of life—and each one of us is a new and unique manifestation of this life. It is this newness, this uniqueness, that we are to bring into the world through our individual lives. And it is also this uniqueness that provides us with what we call "inner guidance."

In the new spiritualism of our times, we find ourselves turning to the teachings of ancient societies that were more intuitive than our own. We do this not because we are seduced by exotic promises from the past, but because it is through the intuitive that we begin to experience the spiritual connection with our fellow beings on this planet. We move from a cerebral or intellectual experience toward a heartfelt one; from the viewpoint of a "detached observer," so important in the scientific tradition, toward a viewpoint of "involvement, commitment, and love."

SELF-KNOWLEDGE—
THE PATH TO SELF-POWER

In this book we'll be talking a lot about self-knowledge. What exactly is self-knowledge? The short answer, in the context of this book, is easy: *Self-knowledge is the awareness of our Inner Self, its greatest gifts and inner powers. It is also the awareness of the other self-limiting forces within us (which we call the Mask Self) that prevent us from fully actualizing our inner gifts and powers.*

For thousands of years, we have known that self-knowledge was the path to personal power. Yet each generation has supported its own taboos against this knowledge. In organized religion, these taboos were supported by threats that you would go to hell if you strayed from the path dictated by the priests and struck out on your own. Public education was and still is supported by grading systems and other competitive measures that teach individuals that there is something wrong with them if they are not just exactly like everyone else. In medicine, even benign processes such as self-exams of the breasts and pelvic and genital areas were once guarded skills of the physicians, putting medical tests above self-discovery and self-responsibility.

Today, the world is opening to a new reality. The doors of the high priests' temples, which have fostered taboos in so many areas of our lives, are flung open. We are insisting on a new democratization, where the tools of empowerment through self-knowledge are available to all. Still, few of us are entirely free of the influences of the high priests, fearful of what might happen were we to challenge the taboos.

We each overcome the taboos against self-knowledge and embrace the Inner Self bit by bit, sometimes gradually, sometimes rapidly. With success and the pleasures of enjoying our new knowledge, there comes a new confidence that we can set aside the taboos and not only survive, but prosper in the process.

As we are told in the *I-Ching*, victory comes only by daring to challenge the dragon. In this case, the dragon is any society's taboos against self-knowledge, combined with the doubts and fears of the Mask Self, while victory is to be found by embracing and learning how we can better trust the guidance of the Inner Self and thus "follow our bliss."

In this book, as in these workshops, we'll be exploring how to use some of our own deepest, happiest, and most profound life experiences as guiding lights. We'll be exploring how certain very subtle feelings are actually steady and powerful beacons, directing us on a life path of self-discovery and self-realization. Through following our bliss in our work and in our relationships, we can reawaken a sense of our own creativity and love of life, which for so many of us has become lost or dulled. We can find a way of life that is meaningful and purposeful, a way of life that *makes your heart sing*, a way of bliss.

—Hal Zina Bennett and Susan J. Sparrow

ONE

What Is Bliss?

Arise and drink your bliss!
For everything that lives is holy.
　　　　　—William Blake

In the past few years, there has been increased interest in the question of what really constitutes "Quality of Life." We have begun placing new emphasis on human values in the workplace and on broadly spiritual values in our personal relations. We have begun to look inward, at our own personal resources and potentials, and at our own loves, fears, and dislikes, for answers to life's most perplexing questions, such as: "How can I enjoy greater intimacy with my friends and family members?" "How can I feel at peace with myself?" "What can I do to feel that my life has meaning or purpose?"

More and more people are coming to recognize that there is a guiding force within each one of us that simply cannot be ignored. That force seems almost deceptively simple at times. The mythologist Joseph Campbell called it our "bliss," and he said that the "ultimate adventure" in all our lives comes when we "embrace our own personal destiny" by following our bliss, that is, by trusting and being guided by *what we love.*

TO YOUR HEALTH, SUCCESS, AND HAPPINESS

Nearly everyone knows what it is to follow one's bliss. It is, for example, the state of being that we experience when we are totally immersed in our work or in a favorite recreational activity. Often we experience it when we're deeply attracted to another person, or even when we're anticipating the purchase of a wonderful object such as a new car or something for our home. It may also be experienced when we follow a "hunch" about contacting a friend, who, it turns out, was only that moment wanting to talk with us. Maybe we experience it when we honor a "gut feeling" we had about a business associate, who later turned out to be untrustworthy. Or maybe we have seen its expression in our "instinct" for choosing exactly the right gift for a loved one.

Less common than these is the experience of feeling that we have a kind of "Homing Device" within us, like the automatic pilot on a great ship.

Imagine that this Homing Device was created around the world's most sophisticated computer, programmed by a staff of the greatest programming geniuses ever known. In fact, both the computer and the programming are advanced so far beyond the capabilities of anything we could even imagine in today's technological world that we really have to think of them as coming from another world, a civilization that is centuries ahead of our own.

Imagine that this computer, which is the hardware serving our inner Homing Device, is capable of reading signals from every sense organ, from each and every part of the brain and nervous system, and from every vital organ we possess. It is capable of understanding our emotions, even the very complex emotions of love. It is just one of the many homeostatic mechanisms we inherit at birth, helping us to protect and heal our body/mind.

The Homing Device of which we speak reads messages from virtually every part of the body and sends signals to the brain in the form of thoughts and emotions. Although the mechanisms for doing all this are in place, most of us have never learned exactly how to make full use of them. Either we don't know how to read the messages our Homing Devices send out or, far more likely, we have been conditioned against paying any attention to these messages. For most of us, it is a little of each.

When we pay attention to our Homing Devices and follow their guidance, we invariably feel great about ourselves and in perfect harmony with the people or activities we're involved with at that moment. Decisions are never difficult because we know where we're heading and why.

People who follow their bliss and trust it as their Homing Device are often very successful in at least one area of their lives: in the area of making money, in the area of having meaningful relationships, in a creative endeavor and so forth. Srully Blotnik, a highly successful Wall Street consultant, once observed that among men and women who were particularly successful at making money, there was "a particularly good match" between their interests and innate abilities and the activities that brought them their fortune.

This "good match" is an important source of commitment. It is the source of what we often call a personal goal or mission. Not only are we motivated by the mission, but that motivation often leads to fulfillment. As Dennis Jaffe and Cynthia Scott put it in their fine book *Take This Job and Love It*, "People who follow a dream or have a deep sense of purpose about their work are rewarded with an almost inexhaustible supply of energy. People moved by this internal energy source are fired up by inspiration. They are likely to find the energy required to finish the difficult, even mundane tasks that go into any achievement."

Here's a true story that helps to illustrate this point: There was a man who, since he was very young, had been intrigued with antique bottles and glassware that he dug up at various historical sights throughout the country. In the beginning, his interest was strictly as a hobbyist, and certainly he had never thought of bottle collecting as a way of making much money.

Over the years, he amassed a huge collection of antique bottles, many of them dug up at construction sites, abandoned houses at "ghost towns," and so forth. He began cataloging his collection, meticulously tracing the history of each object back to its source. His cataloging project became known to other collectors like himself. Soon he found other collectors contacting him from all over the world, turning to him for help in identifying pieces from their own collections. The demand for this man's information became so great that he eventually decided to write a book about it. Almost immediately the book became a success, and a continuing "best-seller" was born.

This single success story is the essence of honoring one's inner guidance and following our bliss. It clearly illustrates how, when we are well matched to our work, numerous facets of ourselves are automatically put into motion. Everything we are finds expression in our work. Parts of ourselves are activated that until then had lain dormant. We seem to succeed almost without effort.

Trusting our own inner guidance, that is, following our bliss, is the key. But we can find the urgency of paying attention to this inner guidance expressed in other ways as well. For example, denying it, not being true to it, or misreading its messages can ultimately produce a sense of dissatisfaction with ourselves, with those around us, and even with life itself. In recent years, medical researchers have shown that when certain kinds of tensions occur, they result in hormonal changes, changes in heart and respiration rates, and changes in blood flow throughout our bodies. Most emotions we experience are actually physical symptoms of these changes.

It is very clear from studying the psychophysiological processes that our denial of messages from our inner homing devices can play a significant role in our health, being a causative factor in most stress-related diseases—everything from tension headaches to certain kinds of heart attacks and cancer.

Many of us become aware of tension messages from our homing devices only at the point when we feel rather advanced physical symptoms. For example, we may get a headache or a stomachache. We may have trouble with our backs or even have heart palpitations or a sense of breathlessness. We may have frequent infections such as colds or flu, or we are accident-prone, hurting our bodies or breaking things around us.

While there can be other causes for these symptoms, they are often nothing more than messages which probably started out as very subtle feelings, such as a sense of doubt or a nagging suspicion or a tiny bit of fear. But for one reason or another, we ignored these messages. When we did not heed them in these early stages, but chose instead to move forward on the same path that triggered them, the uncomfortable messages got stronger. In fact, they slowly evolved from subtle, nagging feelings of discomfort into actual physiological changes, causing increased discomfort and concern.

Many physicians have come to look upon stress-related disease as amplified messages from the frustrated Inner Self. Here we are reminded of the lines from Boris Pasternak's novel *Doctor Zhivago*:

Your health is bound to be affected if, day after day, you say the opposite of what you feel, if you grovel before what you dislike and rejoice at what brings you nothing but misfortune. Our nervous system isn't just a fiction, it's a part of our physical body, and our soul exists in space and is inside us, like the teeth in our mouth. It can't be forever violated with impunity.

So many of us have lost touch with the inner guidance of our own thoughts and feelings. We no longer know how to express those deepest, most creative parts of ourselves which are unique and spirited, making each day exciting yet seeming to simplify our lives. Tensions at work and at home, financial worries, concern about our families, bewilderment about ourselves, everyday news of our troubled world—all these issues seem to throw up barriers to the joy that, deep in our hearts, we know is our true inheritance and birthright. On the positive side, life offers few treasures greater than those we enjoy when we are following our bliss.

HELP FROM THE PAST

The phrase "follow your bliss" speaks to so many of us so strongly. These three words evoke an ancient belief that our hearts tell us is true: that our Inner Selves are somehow very important sources of personal inspiration and guidance. Indeed, when we choose to trust its inspiration and guidance, we discover that the Inner Self is a conduit to a higher power beyond the restrictions of our egos. We discover the very real possibility that we each have a purpose and a mission to be fulfilled, with a meaning that extends beyond our selfish needs and desires. And when we take the next step, to heed the call to express our Inner Selves, we experience a level of personal satisfaction and delight with the mystery of our lives that can be achieved in no other way.

Has there ever been another time in history when so many people have asked so many questions about the nature of the Inner Self? It seems that we have entered a period in human evolution when we are asking for answers beyond those concerned with exploring and controlling the external environment. We are turning to the exploration of the inner world, a world that some say is even more vast and mysterious than the heavens themselves. And what we are finding is that our discoveries of *inner space* are changing our visions of what is real and important in our own lives. It is changing our personal values, the ethics of our daily lives, the ways we relate to ourselves, our life work, to other people, to our environment, and to the universe itself.

It is no accident that at this time in our history, spiritual and scientific thought seem to be coming together. Starting out with very different methods for exploring the nature of life, the two seem to have come to a place of agreement. They are both providing us with a vision that our lives are not simply isolated bits of protoplasm that live for a brief span and then die. Rather, we are each apparently a part of an infinitely large pattern, one whose most elemental parts are something other than matter and energy. For the moment, all this seems beyond the grasp of our logical brains, though somehow not beyond the capacities of our intuition.

As our individual lives are revealed to us as part of a larger plan, we are compelled to look inward for answers. Like biologists seeking the genetic codes within a cell, we seek inwardly for the codes that might tell us how best to fulfill our personal mission.

Throughout history we find endless numbers of references to the conviction that our inner needs, as well as our unique life purpose, will unfold and be revealed to us through our vocations, our relationships with other people, and through our responses to the seemingly mundane matters of our daily lives. The phrase "follow your bliss" reminds us of this ageless wisdom and suggests that maybe our Creator intended us to discover greater, deeper truths about the nature of our individuality, to not be satisfied with only those ways of life suggested by our parents, society, or other institutions.

In this book we take the position that our individuality houses a spiritual truth that is at least as important as recognizing our universal nature beyond the ego. It is a belief that maybe our greatest mission at this time is to look very closely at our own lives in the here and now, at our relationships, and at our vocations. It is a belief that we can best serve ourselves, others around us, other nations, and our planet by taking another look at our inner lives, and by finding new ways to express who we are and what we are about.

Even in reading that simple phrase "follow your bliss," you may be reminded of times in your own life when you followed a gut feeling, a sense of direction that came from your heart, and in doing so, you felt that you had come fully alive. Of one thing you can be sure: The force that guided you at those times came from a very different source than the desire for a better-paying job, a bigger house, or a fancier car. It came from a source that is ageless, a part that we have in common with every person who is, was, or ever will be.

A CLOSER LOOK AT WORK AND RELATIONSHIPS

In the last decade of his life, Sigmund Freud was asked what he felt were the ultimate measures of a successful life. He answered that they could be found by looking at our ability "to work and to love." Few people would deny that these two key areas of our lives—work and relationships—are important. After all, it is here that we give most of our time and energy. And it is through expressing ourselves in these areas that we experience our lives as purposeful, meaningful, and fulfilling. Yet as rewarding as they can sometimes be, work and relationships are also the source of much frustration, conflict, confusion, disappointment, and pain. If we could only learn to follow our bliss in these two areas, we could not ask much more of our lives.

Where do we turn for guidance in work and relationships? Wouldn't it be wonderful if there were one place where we could go for counsel that would really help us solve every problem and tell us how to make the right choices? Working and loving would be so much easier and so much more satisfying then. But we all know it isn't quite that easy.

Someone once said that the trouble with life is that no one knows how to do it quite as well as one would like to. We don't come into being as new cars do, with an operator's manual in the glove compartment. Life, how to live it, is filled with mystery. The only school for learning how to do it is in the living itself, and we seem to begin figuring out how to do it well only after we've gotten at least halfway through it.

In our search for guidance and direction, there is no end of good advice. Friends, parents, therapists, religious and spiritual teachers, books, movies, plays, music, and entertainments all beckon to us, promising a better way. But as often as not, when we attempt to follow these various sources of guidance, we end up juggling a mass of contradictions and mixed messages in our minds. So much advice about living seems to work best for the advice givers themselves, causing us to wonder if the lessons we learn are specific to the individual and rarely transferable to others.

Certainly we've all seen examples of how difficult it is to make meaningful life choices: Our friend Joe accepts a college roommate's invitation to go into business with him and make a lot of money. Having been poor all his life, Joe jumps at the chance, convinced that he has been offered a way to fulfill a lifelong dream. He experiences momentary success, but a few years down the line he says he's caught up in the rat race and is convinced that the business is eating him alive. The money is no longer worth the sacrifice. Similarly, pressed by her fear of being alone after her mother's death, our friend Jane marries a man who offers a home and financial security. He is a kind and generous person, but three years later Jane finds herself bored. She wants a career of her own. She and her husband come to the realization that they have outgrown each other, and after a painful divorce, they go their separate ways.

So many of us are finding that our most successful choices in life come not from following the pull of people, events, or even socioeconomic forces outside us, and not from following our own fears, but from certain promptings that come from deep within us.

There are so many phrases that describe these inner promptings: "follow your bliss," "dancing your inner dance," "living your own life," "doing what makes your heart sing," and "trusting your own rhythm."

Every one of these expressions confirms our belief that there is, deep within us, something that seeks expression, something that asks for recognition. It makes itself known in a thousand different ways: as a certain gut feeling, a pull to experience ourselves as productive, creative, and loving, able to love and be loved, and able to make a contribution that perhaps will be important far beyond the limits of our own lives.

How do we find the "right work" or the "right relationship" or simply the "right action" to satisfy these deep and insistent inner needs? How do we find the life path where we can feel that we can *make a difference*, and truly experience our bliss? The good news is that there is a part within each one of us that can provide the guidance to satisfy our deepest needs in work and relationships. It is a part that, at our birth, we bring into this world for the very first time. While this part is highly individualized and new, it is also universal and ageless, giving us a precious identity that we can share with every other human being, even since the beginning of time, connecting us all as one. When we're in touch with it, life takes on a quiet excitement. This is our bliss, and it is like no other experience we can name. Like an inner compass or the "homing device" on a great ship, it gives us direction and purpose. It provides guidance for every activity in our lives.

If we stop to get in touch with this part, and we learn to trust what it is telling us, we have the sense that we are never alone. Decisions and choices that come from this source seem "positive and right," effortless and natural, with a logic and simplicity that has a beauty all its own. There is never any doubt that our choices and actions make a difference, both to others and to the world around us, and perhaps for generations to come.

Our bliss can help move us forward, providing a positive momentum. When we are following it, it is as if we are energized in a new way. We may even begin to feel that our work is eased and our relationships enhanced by a swift but invisible current that carries us along.

NEW MEANING IN WORK AND RELATIONSHIPS

The inner guidance that comes from following our bliss can extend into every area of our lives, from our first steps as infants to our very last breaths here on Earth. It can direct our decisions in everything from the clothes we put on in the morning to the choices we make in our careers, our personal relationships, our marriages, where we shall live, and how many children we shall have.

We all too often become aware of the importance of our inner guidance only when we have lost touch with it. For example, we might feel that we are not living up to our potential at our jobs. We may feel that we are trading away our lives for a paycheck. Or we might feel empty, unloved, or frustrated in a present relationship. Perhaps we've begun to realize that we are sacrificing our own needs for another person's happiness—a decision that is rarely successful—or that who we truly are is being ignored or "discounted" by others. Whenever these situations arise, most of us feel that our lives lack meaning or purpose. We begin seeking ways to get our lives back on track.

When we are in touch with our own inner guidance, there is always the sense that even when life is most challenging, we still have hope, a *dream*, a *vision* of what our lives can be in the future that is both positive and inspiring. This dream or vision can be such a powerful force! When we open ourselves to it, it guides us forward like a wise and deeply compassionate counselor, helping us to see our own plan for achieving personal fulfillment and meaning. When we're not in touch with our inner guidance, we simply feel lost. Nothing seems quite right to us, and we may even experience a sense of alienation and disorientation. We may begin seeking answers to our life problems in other people, other situations, and even in substitutes for personal fulfillment, such as drugs, overeating, unhealthy relationships, or overwork. Such quests nearly always lead us farther and farther from our Inner Selves.

BLISS, THE CONSTANT GUIDE

Even when following our bliss does not seem to be a part of our daily lives, it is nevertheless a very natural and universal experience. If you stop for a moment and go back in time, you'll probably remember experiences in your past when you felt that you were being completely guided from within, that every move, every decision, every thought you had, came smoothly, easily, and gracefully. There was no need to consciously look outside yourself for answers or cues about what you should do, nor did you need to put any effort into "figuring things out."

Sometimes when we ask people to recall moments such as this from their own lives, their first reaction is that we are describing an experience that is not only unfamiliar to them, but seems almost beyond their reach. What we've found, however, is that we all tend to more easily remember difficult times in our lives, and these can mask over our moments of bliss. In addition, the kinds of experiences we're talking about can be very private and intimate ones for many, many people. As with the most tender experiences of our lives, we recognize that these are delicate and precious memories, not ones that we are willing to risk sharing for fear that we will be criticized, belittled, or that others will simply not value them as much as we do.

Whether we are hiding these experiences from ourselves or protecting them from other people's insensitive reactions, the best way to get in touch with them is to recall them through mental imagery. Let your mind's natural abilities work for you now, bringing these experiences out of your unconscious mind and into your conscious awareness through a few key words. Here's how you can do that:

For a moment, stop and reflect on what the phrase "follow your bliss" means to you. Let yourself recall moments in your life when you were doing something that completely delighted you. As you did this, you may have felt happy, free, and totally at peace. Perhaps you'll remember feeling *at one* with yourself, as if there were no separation between your inner world and the outer one. You may look back at such moments as being times in your life when you were motivated by very different forces than those that ordinarily guide you in your everyday life.

Moments of bliss may have come while walking on the beach during a vacation or after completing a business deal on which you'd been working for many months. Some people describe these moments in almost mystical ways, such as: "I felt that I was being guided by a mysterious force." Others describe them in terms of their own efforts: "It was as though everything I'd worked for was falling into place in one beautiful moment in time." Still others describe them in more everyday terms: "I don't know what happened, but I just felt completely *at peace* with what I was doing." However it is expressed, these are all moments of following your bliss.

For a few moments, allow your memories to bubble forth into your consciousness. Enjoy yourself as you go over any details. You might want to remember the people you were with at the time—if other people were involved at all. You may want to recall the particular landscape, building, or other place where the event took place. Take your time with this. Luxuriate in the memory. And then acknowledge whatever you are experiencing at this moment as being what it's like to follow your bliss.

When we are following our bliss, we truly have access to our self-power. Self-power is like no other form of power in that it does not depend on controlling other people or the external environment. Self-power emanates from within us and is the main source of our self-esteem. When we are embracing this power, we are responsive to the environment, flexible, instinctively knowing the most appropriate thing to do, and completely at peace with the outcome. In religious texts it is often described as "being at One with the Universe or with God"; in athletics it is described as "the sweet spot in time"; people in both the sports and the business worlds refer to it as "the peak performance"; and in psychology it is often called the "peak experience."

From even the most fleeting experiences of bliss, we can begin to see that certain very subtle messages from within us are actually steady and powerful beacons, directing us on a path of self-discovery, self-trust, and self-realization that we can get in no other way. As we discover how to interpret and follow these beacons, we find ourselves reawakening to a sense of our own creativity and love, which may have become lost or dulled by the pressures, frustrations, and sheer bewilderments of our lives.

If it is true that following your bliss is a "natural" part of the human experience, it is also true that most of the time we don't see it as being very important in the normal course of our lives. Bliss seems to occur only serendipitously, and it is not common knowledge that we can turn to our past experiences of it as a dependable resource for making choices and major decisions in our lives. Nevertheless, following our bliss is something we can learn to do deliberately. It is a skill we can develop, like reading or writing or getting good at a favorite sport. Your own deepest, happiest, and most profound life experiences can become trusted beacons for making choices that will bring about the deepest satisfactions and joys that life has to offer, in your life's work, in your relationships, and in the challenges of your daily life. That is the message of this book.

AN EIGHT-STEP PROGRAM

In exploring the skills needed for following your bliss and expressing your gift, we'll be applying what we learn in very practical ways to three key areas of our lives: careers, relationships, and everyday challenges. These are the areas that require the most from us personally, and it is here that we can test our knowledge fully.

In the following pages, we'll be taking you through an eight-step program for following your bliss and using it as a guiding force in your life. These eight steps are:

1. Become Acquainted with the Inner Self
Know how the Inner Self expresses itself and how to sort out which of its messages can help you follow your bliss and which can actually impede you in that goal.

2. Develop Communication with the Inner Self
Expand and develop your present skills for communicating with your Inner Self, amplifying those messages.

3. Embrace Your Gift

Clearly identify and embrace the skiils, knacks, instincts, and "personal loves" that are natural, easy, and pleasurable in your life. These cast a bright light on your gifts, which you'll learn can be focused and applied in many different ways that bring you deep personal fulfillment.

4. Free Yourself from the Mask Self

Some inner messages blind us to our true gifts. These messages come from the Mask Self, which often wants to convince us that following our bliss is dangerous, selfish, or beyond our reach. You automatically diminish the Mask Self's influence by learning to recognize its voice.

5. Understand the Lens of Perception

We each create inner worlds by which we "make sense" of the external world. We call the part of us that does this the "Lens of Perception." It is here that we make the subtle changes necessary for embracing our gift and following our bliss.

6. Heal the Essential Wound

The "Essential Wound" is the foundation of the Mask Self. We heal it through the Lens of Perception, transforming the negative influences of the Mask Self into positive ones that increase our skills, enhance our self-power, and further clear the path for following our bliss.

7. Identify the Characteristics of Your Life Path

The six steps above provide you with highly individualized information about yourself. In this step you put all the pieces together, creating a kind of personalized "map" of your life path, upon which you will travel to follow your bliss.

8. Application

In this, the last step, you'll be applying the "map" you've put together to a real problem or decision in your life. You will then have a concrete experience of how it feels, as well as what you must do to follow your bliss in any situation that arises in the future.

In the following chapter we become acquainted with the key parts of the inner world that we'll be working with in this book. This chapter helps us get focused on the Inner Self, providing an overview of how the gift, the Mask Self, and the Lens of Perception fit in. This is a foundation chapter, upon which you will be building the self-knowledge and skills that will allow you to follow your bliss, using it as the guide to self-realization in your life's work, your relationships, and in the challenges of your daily activities.

As you take this next step, there's a quote we'd like to offer. It was Igor Sikorsky who said: "The work of the individual still remains the spark that moves mankind forward." His words serve to remind us that it is through our individuality, through the expression of the gifts that make us each unique, that all our lives can be improved. We'd like to add that it is also through this path that we come to deeply enjoy our own lives and all of life around us. It is through following our bliss that we find a new depth and love within ourselves that spread out into everything we touch. Expressing our Inner Selves and giving our gift back to the world is an act that will ultimately be rewarded a thousandfold.

TWO

The Peak Experience and the Treasures of the Inner Self

Direct your eye inward, and you'll
   find
A thousand regions in your mind
   Yet undiscovered.
                         —Henry David Thoreau

Some years ago, Michael Toms, the host of "New Dimensions Radio," had a conversation with Joseph Campbell which particularly moved us. As we begin this chapter of our book, that conversation comes back to mind, reminding us of the wealth we each possess in the Inner Self.

During the interview, Joseph had made the comment to Michael that "where you stumble, there your treasure is." The mythologist then dipped back into his storehouse of teaching stories from ancient times to make his point.

In *The Arabian Nights*, Campbell had said, a farmer is

29

plowing a field when the blade of his plow suddenly gets caught on an object planted firmly in the earth. The farmer, who is very annoyed by this, pulls the plow away and reaches down to see what has stopped him. He discovers a huge iron ring, and brushing away the dirt, he finds that it is attached to a door. He pulls hard, the door gives way, and he finds himself staring into a cave filled with magnificent jewels.

In the interview, Campbell goes on to say: "And so it is in our own psyche; our psyche is the cave with all the jewels in it, and it's the fact that we're not letting their energies move us that brings us up short. The world is a match for us, and we're a match for the world. And where it seems most challenging lies the greatest invitation to find deeper and greater powers in ourselves."*

This is such a different view of the Inner Self than most of us are familiar with! So much of the time when we hear the term "Inner Self," we think of the dark unknown, a mysterious and somewhat forbidding place. Some people even associate the Inner Self with evil, with those destructive thoughts and feelings we may harbor but not want to admit that we have.

So many of us have been taught to think of our Inner Selves as something to keep hidden, or as the source of trouble in our lives. Popular interpretations of *psychoanalysis* have contributed much to this false belief. Simplistic views of Freud, for example, lead us to question if there is not a symbolic expression of hostility or "repressed sexuality" behind every dream and slip of the tongue. And no doubt Hollywood has contributed much to this misunderstanding, with otherworldly villains acting out what is frequently depicted as "the dark inner promptings of the soul."

The school of thought that Joseph Campbell and many,

---

*Michael Toms, ed., *An Open Life: Joseph Campbell in Conversation with Michael Toms* (New York: Harper & Row Publishers, 1988). Original tapes later compiled as a book.

many others espouse is something very different. Campbell offers a picture of the Inner Self as a positive force in our lives, the source of light, great energy, and the wellspring of our creativity. He provides us with the picture of the Inner Self not as a source of dark, forbidding mystery, but as the source of our greatest power as individuals. In Joseph Campbell's terms, the Inner Self is the most valuable treasure of all, and when we can allow the energies of this treasure to guide our lives and motivate us, the true wonder of who we are and what our lives can mean opens up to us.

If we had to find a single image to describe the Inner Self, it would have to be a mixed metaphor. On the one hand, the Inner Self is that rich and vast treasure trove described in Campbell's retelling of the *Arabian Nights*. On the other hand, the Inner Self is a guide, constantly beckoning to us, urging us to follow, urging us to grab hold of the iron ring at the door to this treasure trove so that we might fully open up to that greatest of all fortunes, ourselves. When we finally make the decision to pay attention to the guidance of this Inner Self, we truly begin to follow our bliss.

FINDING THE RING AND LIFTING THE DOOR

The American psychologist Abraham Maslow was a pioneer in the study of the positive forces that can be found in the Inner Self. Most psychologists until then had based their work on a medical model. The key of that model was that if one was able to isolate diseased parts and somehow excise them, the person would be made well again. But Maslow saw that this way of looking at human life had clear limitations; it kept both the physician and the patient focused on what was wrong rather than on what was right. Humans being what they are, it was clearly possible to always find a "diseased" part within an individual's psyche. The crusade to search these diseased parts out and excise them might never come to an end.

And after all, wasn't the real point of the healing arts not so much to eradicate disease as it was to create health?

Maslow turned away from the traditional medical model that was focused on disease, and instead focused his attention on what was healthy, on what was right in the individual. For many years he researched the nature of the very highest moments in human experience, moments when the person felt fully actualized, fully utilizing all his or her inner resources as they pertained to a single activity occurring in the moment.

Maslow became very familiar with those moments when people were happiest, when they felt most accomplished and most fulfilled. Taking a scientific approach, he carefully researched his subject, interviewing hundreds of people from all walks of life, in the hope of discovering how these experiences of accomplishment and personal fulfillment affected people's lives. He tried to paint us a picture of what goes on in our minds when we are operating at our very highest levels. He believed that we could learn much more about how the human mind worked if we looked at what was "right" in ourselves rather than looking only at what was wrong.

THE PEAK EXPERIENCE DEFINED

Abraham Maslow listed sixteen qualities that were associated with peak experiences. Although not everyone who Maslow studied reported experiencing all of these qualities, most felt that they had experienced a majority of them. We have abbreviated Maslow's original list for economy's sake.

1. Feelings of being more "whole, unified, and integrated" than usual.
2. Feelings of being more yourself at the same time that there is a feeling of merging with the activity you're involved in at that moment. (While listening to music, for example, you might seem to *become* that music rather than being outside it.)

3. Feelings of utilizing all your capacities to the fullest.

4. A feeling of effortlessness and ease, though working at one's greatest capacities.

5. Feelings of yourself being the prime mover in the present situation, self-determined and self-actualized.

6. Free of blocks, inhibitions, fears, doubts, self-criticism, etc.

7. Spontaneous and expressive, flowing outward, responsive, unrestrained, instinctive, etc.

8. Feelings of molding or creating, interacting with people, materials, and the environment in a harmonious way, fully accepting the realities of everything around you.

9. At the acme of one's uniqueness and individuality.

10. Feelings of being "all there," completely in tune with the *present.*

11. Feelings of being "pure psyche" or spirit.

12. A feeling of absolute completeness at that moment, having no wants or needs, nothing left to be gratified.

13. Expressions and communications at that moment tend to become poetic and rhapsodic.

14. There is often a sense of completion of an act, a closure, a culmination, a climax or catharsis, an emptying or finishing.

15. Playfulness is often an important part of the peak experience, delight, joyfulness, an amusement with both the smallness (weakness) and largeness (strength) of the human being . . . simultaneously childlike and mature.

16. During and after the experience, a sense of being lucky, fortunate, graced, or even a sense that "I don't deserve this."

Perhaps one of the most important discoveries Maslow made was that when we are working at our highest levels, we have a very particular relationship with ourselves and the world around us. The chief characteristic of this relationship is that first and foremost, we are taking direction from our Inner Selves rather than from a person or situation outside us. This does not mean that we aren't being responsive to the external world; on the contrary, we are very much "in the moment," that is, focused on the here and now. For example, a runner might be fully aware of any number of factors while running a race: He or she might be aware of other competitors in the race, the condition of the track, the wind or lack of it, and so forth. But that runner would take direction for how to respond to these factors from deep within him or herself.

While acting at these high levels, the runner is *living completely in the here and now*. There is no sense of separation or detachment from the present—none of that sense of the mind being in one place and the body in the other. Some people described their experiences as something like being on "automatic pilot," guided by a very responsive, accurate, and highly sophisticated source that definitely felt as if it was inside.

Maslow used the terms "core self" and "authentic selfhood" to describe that part of us which is the source of this inner guidance. In his quest to understand the effects of the Inner Self on our lives, he investigated what he called the "peak experience." Although he did not use the word "bliss" in describing his work, peak experiences are, in the context of our present discussion, those moments in life when we are truly following it.

Peak experiences, as he defined them, can occur with any activity, large or small, humble or ambitious, be it physical, mental, spiritual, or simply meeting a practical need of everyday life. They are moments in life when we feel "at one" with the environment and with whatever we are doing. They are moments when everything is working so smoothly and effortlessly, when we do not have to think about what we are doing. People often use words such as "ecstasy" and "sublime" and, yes, even "bliss" when speaking of their peak experiences. In his book *Toward a Psychology of Being*, Maslow described these moments in the following way:

An episode or spurt in which the powers of the person come together in a particularly efficient and intensely enjoyable way, and in which he is more integrated and less split, more open for experience, more idiosyncratic, more perfectly expressive or spontaneous, or fully functioning, more independent of his lower needs, etc. He becomes in these episodes more truly himself, more perfectly actualizing his potentialities, close to the core of his Being, more fully human.

Peak experiences that reveal the powers of the Inner Self do not necessarily occur under positive circumstances. Sometimes they occur when our most heroic efforts are demanded, as when people are overcoming great odds. For example, whenever there is a group of people discussing peak experiences, someone invariably brings up the story of the seventy-five-year-old grandmother who, following a serious traffic accident, lifts a wrecked car to save the life of her injured grandchild. Similarly, in one of our workshops, a rather slight women in her midforties described her own peak experience, which occurred when, in a burst of extraordinary strength, she attacked and frightened off a man twice her size who tried to break into her house.

The important ingredient in these examples of responses to crisis is that under the extreme pressures of saving the life of a loved one, or saving our own life or limb, something extraordinary gets triggered. We suddenly discover powers that we didn't know we had. We become self-directed in the extreme, no longer limited by everyday perceptions about what we are capable or not capable of doing. Ordinarily, seventy-five-year-old grandmothers don't go around lifting cars. And small, unathletic women don't ordinarily counterattack and scare off men who are twice their size. Yet the fact that these things can happen suggests to us that each of us has powers that we hardly ever utilize.

What Maslow discovered was that peak experiences are prime examples of how we feel and act when we are allowing the energies of the Inner Self to move us. They are moments when, for one reason or another, we have access to both physical and mental resources that we hardly knew we had. These moments are the essence of following our bliss. In most positive peak experiences we are following the messages of the Inner Self with such complete trust and confidence that we are hardly aware of doing it. If there is effort involved, it is an effort that teaches us to appreciate our own ultimate capacities.

Maslow was certainly not inventing a new concept. The idea that there was something profound, something deeply moving and important, about acknowledging our inner guidance is many thousands of years old. In the Bible, Paul speaks of the "spirit in the inner man," describing divine guidance as coming through the person's Inner Self, and saying that when we are following that guidance, we are in a state of "grace." But this concept wasn't new to Paul, either.

Six hundred years before Christ, the Chinese philosopher Lao-tzu spoke of the relationship between inner guidance and one's attunement with the Tao. The Tao, he explained, was something like the essence of life itself. He taught that when we found this guidance, we would be unable to see it because we would *be* it; it would be moving in us and through us, just as we moved in and through it. There would be no awareness of separation:

> Meet it and you will not see its face.
> Follow it and you will not see its back.

THE BLISS OF SELF-ACTUALIZATION

Maslow believed that there were certain people who had peak experiences more often than others. These were what he called "self-actualized" people, people who for one reason or another had learned to trust their inner guidance. More accurately, perhaps, they had never been taught *not to trust* it.

Self-actualized people are often ones who look upon their inner guidance as a sort of final authority in making all decisions. This does not necessarily mean that they look upon their inner guidance as all-knowing and all-wise. When they are self-actualized, they do not insist that their own inner guidance is an absolute truth—that is, that it represents a final and complete truth that everyone must follow. Instead, they are firmly convinced that they can only live their lives by taking responsibility for their own beliefs and actions, knowing that they come from within.

We find that people who lack trust in their inner guidance often seek external "proofs" for their choices and decisions. Sometimes, in making choices and decisions, they seek external authorities to back them up: a particular author, a teacher, a parent, a friend, and so forth. They may feel insecure about their choices unless they can line up data to "prove" that they are right.

It is difficult for outer-directed, nonself-actualizing people to accept that there are few absolute truths to help them with day-to-day decisions. While many outer-directed people still had peak experiences, they had them far less often than their self-actualizing counterparts.

Self-actualization is really a matter of degree, that is, all people are more or less capable of it. What's more, we are all capable of learning how to increase our trust in our own inner guidance and become more self-actualizing.

There are two very important points that Maslow's work in this area offers: first, that there really is something within us, a core self, that can provide us with guidance that will lead us to personal fulfillment once we know how to make use of it; and second, that we can experience a significant increase in the emotional and spiritual quality of our lives when we get in touch with this core self and heed the messages it sends us.

Maslow showed that there is great power in allowing ourselves to be fueled by the Inner Self and knowing how to surrender to its guidance. It would appear that when we do trust the Inner Self, we feel better about our lives. We perform better. We are more appreciative of ourselves. We have a greater command of our inner resources and we inspire others around us by providing them with experiences that directly or indirectly celebrate human life.

Both popular and more obscure literature abound with stories that describe the ways our experience of life is enriched at those moments when we are attuned with our Inner Self. Some of our favorite quotes come from athletes, for whom the peak experience of following their bliss is amplified by the fact that it usually involves the full cooperation and coordination of body and mind. One of the best of these quotes is from Roger Bannister, who was the first runner to break the four-minute mile. He recollected that during his record-breaking run, he experienced a sense of complete union with himself and the environment:

> No longer conscious of my movement, I discovered a new unity with nature. I had found a new source of power and beauty, a source I never dreamt existed.

When we witness a peak experience—at a sporting event or a concert or even while doing something as seemingly ordinary as spending a lovely evening with a friend—we get in touch with a sense of wonder that reminds us of our spiritual identity. This deep sense of wonder and appreciation allows us to see our life purpose far and beyond the humdrum routines of everyday life. We escape from the dull realities of the nine-to-five existence, where our lives seem determined by the demands of our jobs, the necessities of paying the bills, and the pressure of living up to other people's expectations of us.

While reflecting on peak experiences, or moments of

following her bliss in her own career, basketball champion Patsy Neal once spoke of moments that went "beyond the human expectation, beyond the physical and emotional ability of the individual. Something *unexplainable* takes over and breathes life into the known life. One stands on the threshold of miracles."

Maslow was by no means the only person during our lifetimes who took note of the powers of the Inner Self. Some years ago, W. Timothy Gallwey wrote a popular book called *The Inner Game of Tennis* in which he explored how the peak experience is expressed in athletic activities. Much of what he had to say in that book is still instructive to us in identifying how it feels when we are trusting our Inner Selves. In the following description of a tennis player who is "on his game," Gallwey reveals much about how the peak experience might feel to us in virtually any activity:

> He's not thinking about how, when or even where to hit the ball. He's not *trying* to hit the ball, and after the shot he doesn't think about how badly or how well he made contact. The ball seems to get hit through an automatic process which doesn't require thought. There may be an awareness of the sight, sound and feel of the ball, and even of the tactical situation, but the player just seems to *know* without thinking what to do.

THE DANCE

As a general rule, peak experiences that acquaint us with our Inner Selves are associated more with the *doing* phase of an experience than with the eventual outcome. In other words, it is in the process of *getting there*, rather than in the final achievement of a singular goal, that we are most in touch with our inner guidance and our bliss. This is not to say that victories and the competition that usually go with them can't be associated with following our bliss. In fact, many professional athletes operate best when there is something at risk—scoring the winning point or ending up on the winning team. But it is not the final score that reveals the heart of the experience to us.

Even professional athletes, whose careers are dependent on their victories on the playing field, recognize there is a difference between winning and having a peak experience. In an article published in *Ms. Magazine* some years ago, Clayton Riley wrote about the beauty he found in watching O. J. Simpson, one of football's greatest running backs. Riley quoted a black friend who said: "White boys only want to know what the final score was; they're only interested in the results. Brothers want to know what happened *in* the game, like, 'Did O.J. *dance?*'" The "dance" he's speaking of is, of course, the peak experience, the moment when the athlete is following his bliss.

Many examples come to mind as we write this, of people in our workshops, or during private consultations, who have recalled moments in their lives when they were following their bliss. The following is the story of a Catholic nun, in her early fifties, a very delightful person who attended one of our workshops:

As children growing up in a remote rural area, Sister Helen and her playmates spent a great deal of time in nature, inventing their own games or simply exploring the countryside. Sister Helen recalled that she found pleasure in being alone. One of her favorite places to go, near her home, was what locals called the frog slough. This was a marsh that was very dark and wet, surrounded by overhanging trees and thick reeds. In young Helen's mind, the marsh was a tremendously alive and mysterious place, rich and primordial in its essence. She loved to go there and listen to the songs of the frogs and birds that made this their home.

The place where she always came to sit by the marsh was a low but dry clearing between two hills. Whenever she approached the marsh, she would begin running as fast as she could. At full speed she would break over the top of the first hill, her feet flying as she rushed headlong toward the marsh. At the bottom of the hill, flushed with the effort and invigorated by the run, she stopped, drew a deep breath, and shouted at the top of her lungs: "God!" Her voice filled the marsh, for a moment there was silence, and then she ran on, bolting up the second hill.

Sometimes she would repeat this exercise several times, each experience more rapturous than the one before, until she was completely exhausted. Then she lay down next to the marsh, bathed in her sense of solitude and ecstasy while she caught her breath.

Although another person might find strong religious overtones in this peak experience, Sister Helen did not see it that way. Instead, she saw it as a time when she was fully expressing, with every muscle in her body, all that she felt she was at that moment. She was expressing her inner nature and experiencing a sense of wholeness and joy. Her running and shouting in the frog slough were deeply personal and, in her mind, had no particular *goal* beyond the experience itself; this was her personal "dance."

WHAT PEAK EXPERIENCES TEACH US

As we've discussed them here, peak experiences as expressions of the great power that becomes available to us when we follow our own inner guidance usually occur within a short span of time—a few seconds, a few minutes, or as long as an hour or two. In this respect, they're important to us only insofar as they provide us with models for following our bliss. They are, in effect, like moments of bliss frozen in time, which allow us, like scientists bending over their microscopes, to look beneath the surface and burst the bubbles of our illusions to discover deeper truths beyond.

Though they are small in scope, we learn from these

fleeting moments of bliss that the same principles which apply to them can also be applied to larger issues in our lives. They can apply to us in choosing a life path, when we make the choice of trusting our Inner Selves to guide us, rather than looking outside ourselves to follow a course that society, our friends, or simply our own fears dictate. The same principles we learn in these models can be applied in our work, in our relationships, and in the ways we handle the routine matters of our daily lives.

Getting in touch with the peak experiences in our own lives is relatively easy. We've included the following exercise as a way of doing this, giving you firsthand knowledge to work from, rather than relying only on our words.

As you begin to recall moments of peak performance in your own life, you move inward. You begin to identify some of the things that guide you from within, that direct you to think and act and feel in one way or another.

EXPERIENTIAL EXERCISE: REMEMBERING PEAK EXPERIENCES

Purpose: The purpose of this exercise is to put you in touch with peak experiences that you have had in your life. You can immediately use your memories of peak experiences as personal resources to help you through difficult periods. In the workbook section in the back of this book, you will be using this same material again, to help you identify important "signposts" to look for in charting the course for following your bliss.

Preparation: Record the following work in a journal, or on paper, where you can later refer back to it. (We'll ask you to come back to this material in the workbook section.)

Instructions: Take a moment to be completely relaxed. To be relaxed and alert, sit with both feet flat on the floor, hands folded in your lap. Close your eyes. Take a deep breath and exhale slowly and gently through your nose. Let your jaw go slack, and be aware of your face becoming softer and more relaxed. Take another deep breath and exhale slowly. This time let your hands and shoulders relax. Be aware of your arms, neck, and upper back becoming softer and more relaxed. Take another deep breath and exhale slowly. Let your stomach muscles relax, and be aware of your chest and belly becoming softer and more relaxed. Take another deep breath and exhale slowly. Let your buttock muscles relax, and be aware of your thighs and lower back becoming softer and more relaxed. Take another deep breath and exhale slowly. Let your feet and ankles relax, and be aware of your calves becoming softer and more relaxed.

For a moment, just allow yourself to luxuriate with this sense of relaxation and ease. Breathe slowly through your nose. Focus your attention on the gentle sensations of the breath moving through your nostrils.

In this relaxed state, recall moments from your past that were particularly pleasurable to you. Happy moments. Moments of ecstasy. Moments when you felt wonderfully pleased with yourself, deeply satisfied with whatever you were doing. You might think of moments when you were in love. Or in your work. Or in a hobby. Or when you were suddenly moved, deep within, by a piece of music, a book, a creative activity, a moment spent in nature, an athletic activity, or a time when you were "just playing" with no particular purpose in mind.

Get in touch with three or four of these events, allowing yourself to thoroughly enjoy these recollections. Then take a moment to record each one briefly. Use two- or three-word descriptions, naming these events so that you can later come back to them. But for now, do not try to record too much detail.

After you've gotten in touch with three or more events, turn your attention to a single one, preferably the one that interests or excites you the most. Look closely at that event. Take note of how you felt at the time it occurred, and try to describe those feelings in a little more detail, using at least a dozen words. Ask yourself how these feelings were different from how you ordinarily feel. In what ways did you perhaps feel like a *different person* while it was occurring?

Let yourself literally bask in the good feelings that you had during these times. Embrace the memories of these events with the confidence that these are important resources of your Inner Self. Since you'll be going back to these events in later parts of this book, take the time to fix them in your mind at this time.

When you are done, simply set your memories of these peak experiences aside for the moment. You do not need to do anything more with them right now. You have completed this short exercise only for the purpose of bringing to your conscious mind an awareness that these peak experiences really do occur in your life.

If, for some reason, you were unable to recall any peak experiences, don't worry. You will be getting another chance later on in the book, and by then you'll have a lot more specific information about making use of the guidance provided by your Inner Self.

MAKING USE OF PEAK EXPERIENCES IN EVERYDAY LIFE

Here's an excellent way to "anchor" these events in your conscious mind and also to begin using them as personal resources right away:

Whenever you are faced with a difficult challenge, or when you are simply feeling pressured, anxious, or depressed, take a moment to recall one or more of your peak experiences. Relax, as you did in the instructions above. Then recall your peak experiences in as much detail as you can. Look upon these memories as positive resources of your Inner Self. By simply bringing them to mind and basking in the feelings that come from them, you create *positive visualizations* which meet specific requirements for you. Take the time to relax. Hold the memories in your mind and you will find that you can increase your confidence, reduce tension, and elevate your mood in nearly any situation.

MOVING FORWARD

In the following chapter, we explore some of the ways that we can communicate with the Inner Self. This includes a discussion of why the Inner Self sometimes seems silent, and what you can do to encourage clearer communication with it. We also provide instructions for getting in touch with your Inner Self through your dreams, your daydreams, and your own *inner guides*.

THREE

The Art of Communicating with the Inner Self

Let the counsel of thine own heart stand.
—Ecclesiasticus 37:13

The American writer Sherwood Anderson once wrote a short story called "The Lost Novel." It was a wonderful tale about a novelist who had spent his life trying to write the perfect book, one that would capture the meaning of his own life and would reveal key truths about all our lives. He was convinced that even though a person might be able to see the truth of his life, no one had ever had the ability to make art of it, to write it down in a way that truly did it justice.

After contemplating all the loves and sorrows of his life, he sat down one night, and in one half-crazed sitting, he wrote a novel. When he finished writing, he believed that he had finally expressed all that he felt within his heart.

Exhausted but deeply satisfied, absolutely convinced that he had just completed the most beautiful piece of literature he had ever written, he got some food and went out for a long walk.

All during his walk, he basked in the wonder of what he had accomplished. He knew the whole vision was there. He knew that he had accomplished what none before him had been able to do. He had written a novel unsurpassed in the way it touched upon the very essence of life.

When he returned to his room, he went immediately to bed and slept soundly until the next morning. When he awoke, he could hardly wait to take up his manuscript and read what he had written. He could picture the entire novel in his mind, all the various bits of dialogue, the relationships between people that he had described, the descriptions of people and places and events that had so dramatically affected him throughout his life.

In the pages of that novel, he had rendered all that he held within his soul, all that his life had been up to that time. All the love he had in his being had gone into that novel. He was convinced that he had done justice to every character and situation, that he had made an artistic breakthrough to reveal truths that no writer before him had ever done. For the first time in his writing career, he felt whole and complete in his accomplishment.

After lying in his bed for some time, the writer got up and went over to his desk. There before him was the stack of papers he had left there the night before. He reached for them, turned over the first sheet, then another and another, only to find what in his heart he had always suspected. He had nothing more than a thick stack of empty sheets!

As Sherwood Anderson told it, the man laughed when he told this story. He was not maudlin in the least. He said only, "I shall never write such a beautiful novel as that one was."

The importance of this story may not be immediately apparent. But with a little probing, we begin to get the lesson Anderson had intended. The *lost novel* is not something that appears on a few sheets of paper bound between the two covers of a book. Rather, it is a vision of life, an understanding, that each one of us possesses within our being. There are times when we can catch brief glimpses of it, when all the characters and situations, all the people and places, conflicts, joys, and celebrations that we have known come together as a whole, providing us with a glimpse of what our lives are all about. The trouble is that this "novel" can never be written down. Although thousands of writers have certainly tried, none has been able to make the vision of his or her whole life fit the constrictions of language.

Although the world of literature has never succeeded in producing such a book, each and every one of us has this "lost novel" within us. For many of us, the glimpses we have of it are so fleeting that we may not have ever dared to imagine that we've really seen what we have seen. At best, it is like a hidden flashbulb going off, perhaps somewhere behind us. Our minds register that we have seen the bright, clear flash of light. And we may even recognize that this bright, clear flash was filled with insight, containing all the knowledge that life has given us. But the vision is so comprehensive that it defies expression.

For our purposes here, the lost novel of Anderson's story represents the world of the Inner Self. It is from this perfect artifact, which exists only within our own consciousnesses, that we take our guidance. It is from this "lost novel" that we take the cues that tell us when we're on our *right path*, following our bliss, and when we are off our path, following a trail that can only lead us further from our life purpose.

Most of us go through our lives never fully aware of this world of the Inner Self. We know there have been

moments of startling clarity in our lives, but holding on to
those moments has been as difficult as trying to pick up a
tiny ball of mercury from the sand. In most cases, we
didn't even know what we were seeing. The clarity came
and went so quickly that it might have been mistaken for
a physiological phenomenon, a twinkling of sensation that
was nothing more than a curiosity.

And so what does all this have to do with "communicating with the Inner Self"? The point is, finally, a simple
one: that there are skills for bringing the lost novel into
focus. The better we know how to apply these skills, the
more we can turn the flashbulb-quick glimpse of our inner
worlds into slow-motion movies of the mind. Knowing
what these skills are, we can finally get our Inner Selves
into focus and tap the rich and vast resources they contain.
Through these skills, we set up our television and communication lines to the Inner Self and start getting familiar with what it has to say.

SETTING UP THE COMMUNICATION LINES

We can follow our bliss only by getting in touch with
its source, and its source is the "lost novel" of the Inner
Self. But how do we do this? How do we communicate
with that part of us which contains the deep resources,
the lost novels, that make each one of us unique? How do
we get in touch with the part that connects us with those
truths that are much larger than ourselves?

In everyday life there really aren't many institutions
that teach or support close communication with our Inner
Selves. Quite to the contrary! As children, we are so often
criticized for doing the very things that would help us stay
in touch with our Inner Selves, to really get to know all
that they offer us in terms of resources that enrich our
lives. We are, for example, discouraged from "daydreaming," making up stories, talking with "imaginary play-

mates," "fantasizing," and so forth, all of which can function as telephone lines for communicating with our Inner
Selves.

Sadly, we find little more support for our Inner Selves
in adulthood. In recent years, there has been an increasing
interest in meditation, affirmations, and mental imagery.
Any of these can be used to help us get to know our Inner
Selves better, yet they are rarely presented this way. One
popular use of meditation, for example, has been as a
technique for reducing stress. But when used for this purpose, it is all too easy to simply shut out our inner wisdom.

Meditation can be a highly effective tool for detaching
ourselves from the perceptions that create stress in our
bodies. But this does not automatically help us to become
better-acquainted with our Inner Selves. On the contrary,
as most of us apply it in modern society, meditation gives
us the ability to actually bypass messages from the Inner
Self. We then continue doing things at our jobs and in our
relationships that our bodies and minds are telling us not
to do. Bear in mind that we are not saying that meditation
only does these things; we are saying that in its most popular forms this is frequently the end result.

Similar blocks to communicating with our Inner Selves
can happen with mental imagery. We might create a "positive image" within our mind, say, as an affirmation to get
a better job or to resolve a conflict in a relationship. But
to be completely effective, that image must speak directly
to our own highly individualized Inner Self. Too often,
ready-made affirmations, positive imagery, and creative
visualizations taken from books or taught in workshops
inspire us for a short time, but we end up being disappointed in the long term. The reason for this is that in
order for it to work well, mental imagery must speak to
the Inner Self very directly and in ways that may be
specific to each person. And there is only one sure way to
create visualizations that do this; we have to know our
unique Inner Selves and what they respond to. A mental

image or affirmation that works for one person does not necessarily work for another. One that is perfectly clear and gets positive results for me may seem like useless gibberish to you. That's just one of the reasons why establishing communication with the Inner Self is so important.

In our workshops, even people who are in the habit of using affirmations or mental imagery and who meditate daily have complained that although they have tried to communicate with their Inner Selves, they really don't feel they make contact. They come away from such efforts feeling frustrated, convinced that the Inner Self simply doesn't exist for them. Nevertheless, we cannot think of a single instance where the person wasn't eventually able to develop very useful and dependable communications with the Inner Self.

LOVE FOR THE INNER SELF

Getting to know our Inner Selves is a lot like getting to know another person. It requires patience, love, and a willingness to listen. Although the Inner Self is really not a separate part of us, treating it as such is often the most effective way to establish the close communication that allows us to follow our bliss. Ultimately, of course, we want to unify the Inner Self with that part of ourselves that we identify with on a daily basis. But just as in a good marriage, unification begins with accepting our separateness and the fact that we each have different ways of looking at the world. We each have different needs and different priorities in life. Clear, patient, and loving communication helps us take the next step, where we find that place in our hearts and minds where we are all one.

As we open communications with the Inner Self, we often find that it is not exactly as we pictured it to be. For the most part, people are pleasantly surprised by what they find. As communications with the Inner Self improve, people discover that what they find there is a source of power and guidance that exceeds even their own wildest dreams. Any fears they might have had quickly dissolve, to be replaced by-feelings of having a new ally, one that is always as close as a thought.

HIDE-AND-SEEK WITH THE INNER SELF

For so many of us, the Inner Self can be like a pouty, belligerent child mumbling incoherently, sending out confused or mixed messages, or simply refusing to show its face. Difficulties in communicating with it are never a case of the Inner Self not being there. It is simply a matter of the Inner Self wanting to be left alone. To communicate with it and begin making sense of its vague or mixed messages, we have only to establish trust, by assuring it that we come to it only with the best of intentions. Just as in dealing with a difficult child, we need to let it know that we are willing to be patient and loving in the process of getting to know it. We need to let it know that we are capable, at least for short periods, of loving it unconditionally, of nurturing its development and growth rather than judging it or trying to make it fit into our preconceived ideas of how we would like it to be.

It was Abraham Maslow's belief that the Inner Self is very powerful, but that it is also "subtle and delicate, very easily drowned out by learning, by cultural expectations, by fear, by disapproval, etc." He did not mean by this that the Inner Self is destroyed by these things. On the contrary, we could not function at all in our lives without an Inner Self. Rather, his point was that the Inner Self could, like a sensitive child, be driven into hiding by certain life experiences. It is almost impossible for us to completely avoid these kinds of repressive experiences in our lives. And so most of us may feel that our Inner Selves are like sulky, fearful children, hiding out, or at least *clamming up*, in an effort to protect themselves.

Because of its subtle and delicate nature, getting in touch with one's Inner Self and staying in touch with it are not always easy. We can lose contact during times when we are having a lot of pressure at our jobs, in our relationships, or even during times when we feel overloaded with everyday responsibilities.

SOMETIMES A WHISPER...

One of the most common ways the Inner Self communicates to us is through what most people call insight. The word clearly describes what is happening at such moments; we are literally receiving "sight" or clarity from within us. For example, you may get an insight that offers a solution to a problem you had struggled with for months. That insight may come at a moment when you least expect it, say, while you are doing something entirely unrelated to that problem.

There are many stories of famous people whose sudden insights provided them with answers that seemed to have eluded them through more analytical methods. One of these is the dream of August von Kekule, the nineteenth-century chemist whose revolutionary insight became a cornerstone of modern chemistry. He was the first to see that the molecules of certain organic compounds are not open structures, but closed rings. He made this discovery while dozing and daydreaming in front of his fireplace. The following is an excerpt from a speech he gave, presenting his discovery to the scientific community:

> I turned my chair to the fire and dozed... the atoms gambolling before my eyes. My mental eye, rendered more acute by repeated visions of this kind, could now distinguish larger structures, of manifold conformation; long

rows, sometimes more closely fitted together; all twining and twisting in snakelike motion. But look! What was that? One of the snakes had seized hold of its own tail, and the form whirled mockingly before my eyes. As if by a flash of lightning, I awoke.... Let us learn to dream, gentlemen.

Here we are reminded of a classic quote from no less than the composer Wolfgang Amadeus Mozart. In the following, he describes how he communicated with his Inner Self and how he saw it as the source of his many creative ideas:

When I am, as it were, completely myself, entirely alone, and of good cheer—say, travelling in a carriage, or walking after a good meal, or during the night when I cannot sleep; it is on such occasions that ideas flow best and most abundantly. Whence and how they come, I know not; nor can I force them.

In quoting Mozart or Kekule, we run the risk of suggesting that messages from the Inner Self, moments of insight that come to us in this way, are exclusive with creative geniuses. But this is by no means the case. These two, one a musical composer, the other a scientist, are simply convenient to quote. They have left behind written memoirs, while other less famous people have not. But millions upon millions of people, whose names we would not recognize, have similar experiences.

Insights are just one way our Inner Selves speak to us. They also speak to us through dreams, fantasy, and make-believe. In fact, for many thousands of years people have looked upon these as some of our clearest expressions of the Inner Self. All our perceptions, be they in the form of wishes, fears, or idle thoughts, are reflections of our Inner Selves. It is as if, in looking very closely at these, we are holding up a mirror, catching the images of what lies within, otherwise hidden from our sight.

OPENING THE WINDOWS TO THE INNER SELF

Dreams and imagination are often called "windows to the inner world." It is from the part of our consciousness that we look upon as "make-believe" or "fantasy" that we recognize the great power of the resources we each hold within us.

Ordinarily we associate dreaming with sleeping. But we actually dream constantly, and this function of consciousness is by no means limited to the nighttime hours, when we shut our eyes and close out the external world. When we are awake, the sights, sounds, smells, tastes, and touch of the physical world demand our attention, causing our dreams to recede into the background of consciousness. When we sleep we isolate ourselves from external stimuli, allowing more of our attention to turn to our dreams.

Even though we may associate dreams with the sleep state, we don't necessarily remember what we dream. If we remember any dreams at all, we remember only the last one or two that we have just before we awaken. The others slip away from us, back into memory. Some people recall their dreams easily and in great detail. But for most of us, getting in touch with our dreams takes some practice.

The easiest way to start opening these windows to your Inner Self is by getting acquainted with the dreams you have in your waking state. You can do this right now. For just a moment, close your eyes. Take a few deep breaths, then exhale through your nose slowly and gently, allowing yourself to relax. After a minute or so, let the focus of your attention turn away from the sights and sounds of the physical world and turn toward what's going on inside your head.

Some people will immediately have a mental picture of something that happened in the past, or of something that they'd like to happen in the future. Others may start thinking about something that they need to do before the day is over. Others may have strong feelings, suddenly finding themselves going back over a situation from the past that was pleasant, or one where they still feel conflict, pain, anger, or regret.

We seldom take the time in our busy lives to fully acknowledge the source of these daydreams, thoughts, and feelings. But following our bliss depends on our doing this. Remind yourself at this moment that these experiences are all coming from within, from our own Inner Selves. Although we may attach many of our thoughts and feelings to people and events in the physical world outside us, they really are, first and foremost, our own creations, emanating from our Inner Selves. Don't get us wrong; we are not saying that we are responsible for creating everything in the external world. We are saying, instead, that how we interpret that world, how we make sense of it, the ways that we have of giving it meaning—all these are functions of our Inner Selves.

Any thoughts and feelings you experience in this area are the stuff of dreams, and all are expressions of your Inner Self. In our waking state the contents of our daydreams may seem abstract and elusive. But in the sleep state the human consciousness has the ability to translate all these thoughts and feelings and sensations into stories where we find ourselves interacting with other people, or walking along a beautiful path in the woods, or driving in our cars, and so forth. In our sleep, we are participating fully in that world of the "lost novel" described in the Sherwood Anderson story we paraphrased at the beginning of this chapter. It is as though we have within us an ability to transform any important theme in our lives into dream stories, where our conflicts or confusions are recorded in vignettes filled with codes and symbols.

ON THE USE OF OUR DREAMS

Of what use are our dreams? The most poignant example I (Hal) can give occurred at the time of my father's death, several years ago. I was in California, he in Michigan, when I got the news that he was in the hospital and that he had only a few days to live. Very distraught, I went to my office, where I found myself looking through journals that I had kept of my dreams over the past several years.

In one of the journals I found the record of a dream about my father's death, which I'd had a few years before. In the dream, I was at my father's bedside, sitting with him in the last hours of his life. I had taken on a very different sort of identity than was familiar to me. My dream self knew everything there was to know about death and the dying process, and this self had complete confidence in his role as a guide for the dying person.

In the dream I also had a helper. It was as though I was his apprentice in this very strange new role. As I read the dream once again, I pretended that my helper was real, that I could talk to him and he would provide me with any information I needed. I asked him what the dream meant, and he said that it meant I was to go back to Michigan and act as my father's guide and helper in his transition from life.

I was horrified by this prospect and I protested, saying I knew nothing about any of this and I didn't want anything to do with it. The dream helper told me that I had nothing to worry about. He insisted that the fact was that I actually knew quite a bit about death, having had a near-death experience when I was a teenager. I could not argue with this. As a teenager, I had been in a deep coma for several days and had felt myself leaving my body and slipping off into a tunnel of brilliant light. Many years

later, a psychologist I was working with explained that
this was what researchers were now calling "near-death
experiences." People who died and then were brought
back to life by doctors often reported them, and it was
thought that this was probably a fairly universal part of
dying.

I asked my dream helper what I should do for my father. He said only that I would get all the help I needed
along the way, both from my dreams and from "regular
people" in the physical world. I had only to trust my
dream and it would guide me. It contained information
from my Inner Self that was too important to ignore. I
asked my helper for confirmation of all this. In my mind's
eye I saw him dramatically raise one finger high in the
air, and with a thick, Dracula-movie accent he said, "You
vill zoon meet an older voman who vill tell you all you
need to know."

I was offended and embarrassed by this. It was as
though my dream figure was making a mockery of my
father's passing, mixing that event with scenes from bad
movies. I also felt that my dream helper was somehow
making a joke at my expense. Nevertheless, I decided I
would take my dream seriously and use it whenever it
seemed appropriate. After all, I had nothing to lose, having no one around me at that moment who could offer me
any better counsel.

I picked up the phone and made reservations to fly back
to Michigan. A couple of hours later I went down to the
travel agency to pick up my tickets. On the way out I
literally bumped into an older woman. I did not recognize
her at first. Then she spoke my name, with the same thick
accent that my dream helper had used. She was a real
estate agent who had sold me a house several years before
this. She asked where I was going, and I immediately told
her.

"Hal," she said, "you *must* come with me this moment.
I have something very important to tell you."

Remembering my own dream and my imaginary conversation with my helper, I did exactly as she said. We went to her office, a few doors from the travel agency. She had me sit down, got me a cup of coffee, and proceeded to tell me that her own father had died of exactly the same disease that my father had. She had sat with him around the clock, until he drew his last breath.

In great detail, she told me everything I needed to know to be helpful to my father during this time. She had information about the physiological and the emotional problems that would arise as my father's disease progressed, and what I could do to be helpful to him where these were concerned.

After leaving her office, I felt well prepared for meeting the challenge that lay ahead. Moreover, I had to ask myself if it was only a coincidence that my dream helper had told me of the "older woman" who would counsel me, and that he had told me about her with an accent much like hers. I do know that if he hadn't done this, I probably wouldn't have taken my bumping into the real estate woman quite so seriously. The similarity of accents had been like a red flag going up, telling me to take a closer look at what was happening in my life at that moment. In any case, I felt that I had been given confirmation that my dream of my father's death could be used as a model for what I should do and how I could best serve him.

In the next two weeks my mother, my brothers, and I sat by my father's bedside. I felt that I was able to help make his passing as comfortable as possible, although there were a great many times when I felt completely out of my depth. At these times, I went back to my memories of the dream, or I asked for counsel from the dream figure. The help I requested was always there, sometimes in the form of moral support, sometimes in the form of practical suggestions, but always with a certainty and calm that gave me courage that I feel I would not have had otherwise.

* * *

In everyday life, we don't often turn to our dreams in the way revealed in this story. Perhaps the most important part of my anecdote is not that the dream was prophetic, but that it allowed me to recognize my own inner resources. In this story we can at least assume that my knowledge of death, which I had gleaned from my own near-death experience, had been stored in parts of my mind that were not easily accessible in my waking state. Through my dreams, I was able to access this knowledge and apply it to my father's death. The dream clearly was an opening, a window that allowed me to make contact with my Inner Self and make use of resources that might otherwise have lain hidden.

ACCESSING THE INNER WORLD THROUGH DAYDREAMS

We often overlook the value of daydreams, passing them off as the aimless wandering of our minds. However, daydreams originate with the Inner Self, and since they are often more immediately accessible than the dreams we have at night, they can be particularly valuable to us. They are like smaller windows that allow us to get fleeting glimpses of the inner self.

Nearly everyone daydreams when bored or mildly anxious. Sometimes it's a way to mentally rehearse a difficult challenge that we know is coming up in our lives. Sometimes it's a way of rethinking something that has happened to us in the past. The most common example of the latter is when we daydream about all the things we *should have said* after an argument.

In recent years, athletic trainers have developed techniques for mentally rehearsing physical movements that require a high degree of accuracy. They have discovered that everyone automatically does this to some degree, but that ability can also be expanded to refine athletic performances of every kind.

We also use our daydreams as a way to plan for the future. How many times have you found yourself daydreaming about a home you would like to own, or a new car you want to buy, or perhaps a vacation trip you want to take? We also use our daydreams to help us find more creative ways of dealing with our relationships and in our quests for personal growth.

Keep in mind that your Inner Self is the creator of all daydreams. The Inner Self is the source, no matter what the subject of the daydream happens to be. And the daydream can tell you as much about your Inner Self as it tells you about the subject it is exploring.

Most of us daydream while waiting in line at the supermarket or while stopped in freeway traffic. We may also daydream while sitting in a crowd of people on a bus or while sitting in the reception room at our doctor's office. At such times we turn inward, going into our own private world. Although we're aware of the outside world, it is this private inner world that has most of our attention.

Daydreams are most active during periods of change or stress in our lives. That stress can be focused on a difficult situation such as getting fired from a job or breaking up a relationship. It can also be around a positive event such as getting married, having a new baby in the house, or changing jobs. Apparently we all use our daydreams during these periods of time to seek solutions and alternatives that will bring us greater peace of mind.

Whenever you are faced with the stress of change in your life, use that time as an opportunity to pay attention to your daydreams as messages from your Inner Self. Whenever you find yourself daydreaming, first make sure that it is safe to do so—i.e., staying alert in traffic around you if you're waiting at a stoplight, etc.—and then allow your mind to drift. Pay attention to the images that flow through your mind.

Develop an *observer mind* as you focus your attention

on your daydreams. The observer mind is that part of you which watches, making mental notes of whatever you are doing even while you are doing it. It is the part that keeps an eye on what's happening around you, and it is also the part that sometimes judges you: "That was great!" or "That was a pretty dumb move!"

Let this observer mind watch the daydream, then ask it to read the daydream back to you in a way that puts it in the *voice* of your Inner Self. Here's an example of how to do that: Let's say you were daydreaming about taking a vacation to the islands. Note this and then mentally verbalize the observation by saying, "My Inner Self created a picture of me lying on a beautiful white, sandy beach in Bermuda, with the warm sun beating down on me."

You might also make mental notes about what your Inner Self must be feeling toward you as it creates these images. For example, in reflecting on your Inner Self's image of the beach in Bermuda, you might comment to yourself: "My Inner Self must think a lot of me. It wants me to take a vacation and enjoy myself."

Ideally, you'd write down your daydreams and your observer self's comments about the Inner Self. Some people do this with long, detailed entries. Others do it with brief two- or three-word reminders. However you choose to do it, this written record provides you with tangible "proof" of your communication with the Inner Self. It is most helpful to make notes on subjects such as the following:

- Where the event depicted in the daydream took place.
- Whether you were alone or with other people.
- The activity you were engaged in.
- Your general attitudes, thoughts, or feelings at that moment.
- Any challenge that was presented in the daydream.

- How the daydream ended.
- How you felt after the daydream ended.
- Observations about your Inner Self's thoughts or feelings toward you.
- Whether or not the activities depicted in the daydream were brand-new to you or were recurring images.
- Any theories you might have about why you had this particular daydream, that is, how it relates to something that is happening in your life right now.
- You might want to try striking up an imaginary conversation with any characters who appeared in these daydreams. Ask them anything you wish, especially as it relates to any source of stress in your life.

Often, as we work with our daydreams in this way, knowing that they are communications with the Inner Self, we come up with some very solid insights and ideas for solving problems we may be facing. Whenever this happens to you, make note of it. Give yourself credit for improving communication with your Inner Self—and give yourself credit for having valuable inner resources.

As you work with your daydreams in this way, the process will probably seem quite familiar to you. It is familiar because it follows our natural abilities. What is different is that you are becoming more conscious of the process. You are seeing how your daydreams are ways to communicate with your Inner Self. And the more you work with your daydreams, the more you'll see that you can make this communication with your Inner Self a very conscious and deliberate thing. Instead of seeing your daydreams as nothing more than your mind drifting, you begin to see them as mental tools for developing a closer and closer relationship with your Inner Self.

INNER GUIDES AND SPIRIT COUNSELORS

Toward the end of his life, the noted psychologist C. G. Jung paid homage to a series of what he called "dreams and fantasies" that he had throughout his life. In particular, he gave credit to a fantasy figure he called Philemon. Philemon had been like a personal counselor who came to him throughout most of his adult life. In his youth, Jung self-published a collection of the conversations he had had with other fantasy figures, in a small book that he titled *Septem Sermones*. In the following paragraph from his memoirs, Jung makes it very clear that he had seen his life as having been directed by the valuable communications he'd established with these figures from his inner world:

> All my works, all my creative activity, has come from those initial fantasies and dreams which began in 1912, almost fifty years ago. Everything that I accomplished in later life was already contained in them, although at first only in the form of emotions and images.

Even though he was highly respected throughout the world, Jung was something of a renegade in his field because he looked for answers outside the European tradition. He was profoundly influenced by ancient cultures since they offered much knowledge about the intuitive side of life, an area that was shunned by most European scholars of his time. In recent years, we've begun taking a second look at these intuitive traditions, acknowledging that their methods for accessing the wisdom of the Inner Self were quite advanced and have much to teach us today.

There is plenty of evidence that Jung had studied the shamanic traditions (he interviewed medicine men in both

Africa and America) and the eastern mystical traditions (he was a close friend of Gandhi's and interviewed a number of Indian gurus). Within these traditions, communication with the Inner Self is revered. It is considered to be a key for gaining understanding about every aspect of our lives, and one of the most valuable sources of knowledge available to us for our personal growth.

Jung relates one very interesting story about his encounter with an Indian guru who was a close friend of Gandhi's. Jung asked this man where he had received his own spiritual teachings. The man answered that his teacher had been a famous Indian spiritual teacher with whom Jung was familiar. The only trouble was that this person had been dead for centuries. Jung then commented on this, saying that he was familiar with the teachings of this man and that he knew this person was dead.

"Yes," the man replied. "Some of us have teachers who are spirits."

Jung concluded from this and similar experiences he had in this realm that there are many things about our own consciousnesses that we don't understand. When we speak of the inner world or the Inner Self, we perhaps are speaking of a part of our consciousness that is not limited by time or space. Through it we are able to escape the finite world, represented by our physical bodies, and for a moment link up with the infinite universe, where, scientists tell us, all is pure energy, existing in timelessness.

SPEAKING WITH MANY VOICES

Within the intuitive traditions, the Inner Self is often described as embodying more than one *persona* or character. In fact, many descriptions of the Inner Self—as in Sherwood Anderson's story—read almost like novels, with different characters appearing from time to time to give advice, to entertain, or even to create conflicts that can deepen our knowledge of life and of ourselves. In the following quote, from the Northern Cheyenne philosopher and medicine man Hyemeyohsts Storm, we have one description of how a variety of *personae* are expressed within the Inner Self of a single person:

> Within every man there is the Reflection of a Woman, and within every woman there is the Reflection of a Man. Within every man and women there is also the Reflection of an Old Man, an Old Woman, a Little Boy and a Little Girl.

ARE INNER GUIDES REALLY SEPARATE FROM US?

In the past few years, there has been much interest in inner guides. We call our communication with them "channeling," and for many proponents of this practice, the guides are entities that exist on a "spiritual plane" outside our own consciousness. But of course, there is a great deal of debate about this. Do the guides have an existence outside the channel's consciousness, or are they a product of the channeler's consciousness?

An entire book could be devoted to attempting to answer this question. Certainly there have been many highly regarded professionals, C. G. Jung included, who felt that their guides had lives of their own. Jung contended that these guides "were nothing metaphysical," but he admitted that they were "as rich and strange as the world itself." In communicating with his inner guide called Philemon, Jung said the following:

> I observed clearly that it was he who spoke, not I. He said I treated thoughts as though I generated them myself, but in his view thoughts were like animals in the forest, or people in a room, or birds in the air, and added, "If you

should see people in a room, or birds in the air, you would not think that you had made those people, or that you were responsible for them."

There have been just as many people who find inner guides invaluable for communicating with their Inner Selves and gaining self-knowledge but who feel that the guides are creations of their own consciousnesses. For us, determining whether or not our inner guides have a reality separate from our own is less important than recognizing that regardless of their nature, many people find them helpful. Whether real or fictional, they appear to be effective for accessing the resources of the Inner Self and assisting us in following our bliss.

Many years ago, Jane Roberts (author of the "Seth" material) called her books novels. She said that the guides who helped her write them were "not higher authorities outside me but provided knowledge that might otherwise not be available."

The use of inner guides is probably as old as human consciousness itself. It is a part of the ancient theater and storytelling traditions, which have been valued in every society as a way of revealing truths that can't be communicated in more linear terms.

In mask and storytelling traditions, storytellers or actors take on characters that are not themselves. Sometimes they wear ceremonial garb and masks to depict these assumed characters, and when they do, something almost magical begins to happen. The actors or storytellers seem to suspend their own egos and for a time take on another identity.

With ego suspended, everyday perceptions dissolved, and both performers and spectators became open to higher truths than what they might have been able to articulate on their own. It is as though we begin communicating with that part of our Inner Selves which is universal, connecting us all as one. Perhaps it is what theologians call *Logos*. In the Bible, the Gospel of John tells us:

When all things began, the Word (Logos) already was. The
Word dwelt with God, and what God was, the Word was.
The Word, then was with God at the beginning, and
through him all things came to be; no single thing was
created without him. All that came to be was alive with
his life, and that life was the light of men." (Oxford, New
English Bible)

There are some who look upon the word of their inner
guides as infallible. We don't subscribe to this theory at
all. The fact is that to seek "ultimate authority" in anyone,
even in the most esteemed spiritual leader, is dangerous.
If we're to truly learn to follow our bliss, we must accept
responsibility for our own consciousness. Whether we are
interacting with a person as real as ourselves or as etheric
as an inner guide, the issue is always the same; we cannot
take charge of our own lives until we take responsibility
for what we bring into our consciousnesses.

There is a wonderful story told by the Native American
teacher Sun Bear. When he first began working with inner
guides, he blindly followed the advice of one, believing
that its wisdom was infallible. After all, this guide was a
deceased shaman whose wisdom had been trusted for generations upon generations. Who, then, he reasoned, was
he to question this man? But, as it turned out, this guide's
advice got Sun Bear into a lot of trouble. He went to his
teacher and told him about this, admitting that he was
quite bewildered. His teacher told him that regardless of
the source of the information, we should never try to make
another person responsible for our own actions. As to the
fallibility of inner guides, Sun Bear's teacher told him:
"Dead don't make you smart."

COMMUNICATING WITH INNER GUIDES

As in the section you just read on daydreams, anyone
can develop skills for working with one's own inner guide
or spirit helper. There are a number of excellent books

available that tell how to do this. You'll find them listed in our annotated bibliography at the back of this book. In the meantime, you might want to experiment by communicating with dream or fantasy figures who have already appeared in your life.

Many people start by going back to childhood experiences. You may have had an imaginary playmate when you were a child. Or perhaps you had a doll or a favorite pet with whom you carried on long imaginary conversations whenever you were lonely or troubled. If you did, bring them back to mind and ask them any questions that come to you. Then sit back in a relaxed and quiet way and wait for answers. These may come to you as thoughts, feelings, or insights. Some people have kinesthetic responses, that is, physical sensations that they associate with pleasure or pain. Each person has his or her own particular style for communicating with inner guides.

One way that we experience these fantasy figures is in the shape of a real person. Maybe you can remember a time in your life when you were all alone, faced with a problem or a conflict and feeling that you had nowhere to turn for help. At such times, you might have thought about a friend, relative, or even a favorite character from a novel you'd read or a movie you'd seen. This could have been a person who was either living or dead, real or fictional. You might have thought, "What would they do in my situation?" Sometimes, without even thinking about it, you imagined an answer: "Of course, they would have done such and such," and that thought would have helped you find a solution to the problem you were facing.

We were surprised one day in a workshop when a women in her early sixties, who had been very successful in the financial world, shared the story of her inner guide. In this case, the guide was the Cowardly Lion from *The Wizard of Oz*. The woman's own lion was very wise, however, and whenever she wanted help with a decision, she simply closed her eyes and imagined him sitting on her desk.

Native Americans had fetish figures and animal totems with whom they communicated in ways very similar to what we've outlined above. Usually these figures were part of their cultural heritage. For example, the Zuni Indians were hunters, and their fetish figures were usually representations of animals that they hunted or which also hunted the animals they did: bears, coyotes, mountain lions, and so forth. As they communicated with these fetishes, they also accessed everything stored in their own consciousnesses about these animals.

You might like to try working with your own fetish figures—objects, amulets, pictures of favorite people living or dead, a doll, a figure of an animal, and so forth. Simply be relaxed, open, and playful as you do this. Initiate conversations with them just as you would converse with a friend. Then wait for the responses that come back to you through your own consciousness.

In the beginning you may feel foolish doing these things, but in time, especially when you enjoy positive results, you'll see that they really do work. At times they seem to have their own identities, separate from our own. At other times they seem clearly to be extensions of ourselves. At times you may even feel that you are *making them up*, just as you'd make up a character for a book if you were writing a short story or a novel. In each and every case, however, we draw closer to the Inner Self. (Readers who wish to pursue this process further might wish to read *Inner Guides, Visions, Dreams, and Dr. Einstein*, by Hal Zina Bennett, Ph.D., published in 1986 by Celestial Arts, Berkeley, CA.)

One of our clients is the vice president of a very large manufacturing company. When she feels the need to communicate with her Inner Self, she closes her office doors, shuts her eyes, and opens up a conversation with "Sara." Sara is a composite fantasy figure who appeared to her one day, partly like her dead grandmother and partly like a character from a favorite novel that she'd read as a girl. Unbeknownst to the company's board of directors, Sara has been their consultant on some very high level decisions. And so far, she has a pretty good success record.

BEWILDERING CHOICES CLARIFIED

Like so many other people we have met, we have learned that in following our inner guidance, we are all faced with an often bewildering array of choices. And like most people, there have been many times when we have followed inner promptings that seemed very important and clear at the time. We may have felt compelled to move to a certain town or to spend more time with a certain person or to take a particular job. But acting upon these promptings ultimately resulted in pain and confusion. And when we now look back at those times, we have to stop and ask ourselves, "Were those choices really necessary? Did they teach us anything that could later be applied in more constructive ways in our lives?"

What we began to see was that there truly are most valuable but subtle lessons to be learned from everything we encounter. On the broadest scale, we have seen that as we attempt to follow our inner guidance, we discover that there are often many voices from which to choose, not just one. And while it's happening, one voice can be just as urgent and compelling as another. Sometimes the inner promptings we experience can be like a chorus of voices, each one urging us to fulfill its wishes. We find ourselves asking, "Which one should I follow in order to follow my bliss?" If we tried to do everything that our inner guidance urged us to do, we might quickly see that we could end up in endless conflict, mentally juggling contradictions and conflicting interests that could literally drive us crazy. So the question is, how do we decide which inner messages to follow? How do we sort it all out?

One of the first things we looked at was whether or not there was any way to distinguish between those voices that simplified our lives and those that ultimately created conflict, disappointment, or anxiety. Were some of these inner promptings more dependable than others? Was it possible to predict which ones would lead us closer to our path, closer to our bliss, and which ones would take us down blind alleys? How could we make sense of the often bewildering feelings we experienced whenever we were faced with difficult choices?

As we compared notes, it seemed to us that there were at least a few indicators to look for, signs that would tell us when we were on the right path and signs that would tell us when we were in danger of getting off that path. For example, it became very clear to us that there had always been a distinct difference in the *quality* of the messages we received from the Inner Self. By quality, we mean *the way in which it was communicated rather than the content of the message itself.*

If actual voices had been involved, we'd describe the differences in qualities as differences in tone and inflection. In other words, it was not *what* the Inner Self said so much as *how* it said it. It's much like that in personal relationships: When a person tells us "I love you," it is the tone and inflection, even more than the words themselves, that can reach out and touch our hearts. *How* they say what they say tells us what is truly in their hearts. And it is that tone and inflection, not the words, that we seek as proof of our bond.

For most of us, it takes nearly a lifetime to develop skills in reading the *qualities* of our own inner promptings. There aren't any classes teaching this, as there are classes for learning to read, write, and do arithmetic. And yet, what could be more important if we are to learn how to follow our bliss?

We began to look for ways to define the qualities that distinguished a trustworthy and positive message of the Inner Self from those which were less trustworthy or which were downright negative. We agreed that for both of us, messages of inner guidance that had the quality of "quiet excitement," of peace, inner calm, and confidence, seemed to be the most trustworthy and the most directly beneficial. When we paid attention to these messages and acted upon them, we found ourselves closer to a life path that truly felt right for us.

The messages that led us off our paths had very different qualities. Describing those qualities isn't easy. Sometimes they had a particular urgency, like a spoiled child pulling at our hand and crying, "Gimme, gimme, gimme!" It was as though the whole world would end if we failed to satisfy those needs *right now*. If there was excitement in the message, it was not the quiet, peaceful, and *centered* feeling of excitement that we experienced when we were on our path; rather, it was the excitement associated with anxiety. It was the "jangly" excitement that goes along with high-adrenaline states. As often as not, when we looked very closely, we'd find fear involved: fear of something happening or fear that we would not be able to have something that for the moment we were absolutely convinced we must have.

As we took a look at all these things, we began to see that at least half the trick of knowing how to trust our inner guidance is really one of learning how to listen for these subtle qualities of tone and inflection. The other half is that most of us have actually been taught to *distrust* what comes from within us. Perhaps in our early lives our own inner guidance was neither supported nor encouraged. For most of us, regaining trust in that guidance isn't easy—not only because we have forgotten how its messages sound, but because we still are haunted by the possibility that we are doing something wrong by following this guidance. Certainly we must come to terms with this if we hope to learn how to follow our own guidance, and in this book, we describe exactly how this is done in the chapter on the Mask Self.

MOVING FORWARD

In all our work with dreams, daydreams, and inner guides, we begin to appreciate the wealth of information that we have within us. Many metaphors have been used by writers over the years to describe these phenomena and what they mean in our lives. They have been described as "mirrors of the soul," meaning that our dreams and visions tell us something about the very deepest parts of our beings. We can also look upon our dreams and visions as being projections of our Inner Selves. They are our perceptions, made into mental movies, and just as a movie or any other art form can reveal something about its maker, so our mental movies can reveal something to us about our Inner Selves.

In the following chapter, we'll be exploring the *Gift*. The Gift comes to us from the Inner Self, and it is through our dreams and visions, as well as our actions in the physical world, that it is fully revealed to us.

FOUR

Discovering the Gift

I am certain of nothing but the holiness of the heart's affections and the truth of imagination....
—John Keats

Throughout folklore and mythology, there is expressed the idea that each and every one of us possesses a "gift," usually described as a knack or natural ability in a particular activity. If you stop to think about the times in the past when you have heard this expression, or you have used it yourself, you'll probably begin to see that it is quite rich in its implications. For example, if we were to say that Jessica is a gifted tuba player, we would generally mean not only that she has a natural ability for playing that instrument, but that she brings something special to her playing of it, something that distinguishes her from other tuba players.

So the gift is not just the raw skill for tuba playing—or whatever your particular gift might be. Much more than this, the raw skill gives Jessica a vehicle for expressing whatever it is that distinguishes her tuba playing from everyone else's. As jazz musicians are fond of saying, "It ain't *what* you do; it's *how you do it* that counts." It's this *how you do it* that we'll explore in this chapter. It's *how you do it* that is truly your gift.

As we use the term here, your "gift" is highly individualized, comprised of everything you bring to every personal expression. It is your innate talents and abilities. It is your unique history, your personal psychology. It is the skills and knowledge you have acquired through your own conscious efforts, as well as the less conscious ones. It is your vision of yourself and the world, your feelings about your life and your relationships to everything around you—all these shaped and molded, at least in part, by your particular life experiences. It is, in short, everything that makes you uniquely you, a being not quite like any other that has gone before you, and not quite like any other that is yet to come.

It is interesting to note that in many of the Native American traditions, there are some brilliantly clear descriptions of this gift. The Hopis, for example, believe that at birth each person is given a particular gift by the Creator, and one's mission in life is to express that gift and bring it into being in his or her lifetime. This is, of course, done through our life work and in our relationships with our planet and the people around us.

It is the Hopis' belief that in the eyes of the Creator, our bringing forth our gift in our lifetimes is absolutely essential for making the universe whole and complete at that point in time. In a very real way, we express our gift not so much for ourselves as for a higher good that perhaps none of us can clearly see or understand. In the eyes of the Creator, each person's gift is equally important, even though one person's might be to rule a nation while another's is to shape simple pots from clay, and still another's might be to raise a family. Rulers, potters, and homemakers are all necessary in life, and one person's life task is no less necessary than any other.

People who follow their inner guidance often report that the activity through which they best express themselves is something that has interested them for a very long time. For example, an architect-builder we interviewed said, "I cannot remember a time that I wasn't fascinated with building things. As a child, I was always experimenting with different sorts of materials—blocks and Legos when I was really small, then tree houses and huts when I was older."

This does not mean that you are without a gift if you feel that there has never been anything that consistently interested you in these ways. A prime example of this was the woman from one of our workshops who, in her fifty-third year, was given a computer by her brother when he upgraded his office accounting system. At first she was intimidated by the machine, but when she saw what it could do and then suddenly caught on to the basic principles of how it worked, her interest was piqued. She signed up for some computer classes at night school, which got her interested in programming. Within the short span of three years, she moved from being "computer-illiterate" to being a gifted computer expert, with her own consulting firm.

What makes this woman's success story especially unusual is that she had grown up prior to the computer age. Obviously, she could not have developed an early interest in computers per se since they were not around when she was a child. However, as she explored the question of what she found so deeply satisfying in computer programming, she recalled that she had always been interested in creating games. In high school she had even invented a board game for teaching mathematics that was later purchased by an educational publisher. Somehow, she said, the programming was the perfect vehicle for her, satisfying this early interest and gift for creating games.

What's particularly important to understand in this story is that the actual vehicle for the gift—be it a tuba, a computer, building toy houses with plastic blocks, running the United States government, or whatever—is not what we are looking for. Rather, we are looking for something that might be described as nothing more than an "affinity" for an activity. In the story of the computer programmer, it was not her affinity for computers so much as her affinity for the kinds of things computers do that attracted her to them. The computer was important only insofar as it provided a *medium* for her to express her gift.

IN SEARCH OF THE MORE ELUSIVE PARTS OF THE GIFT

The gift may make itself known to us as a feeling of being strongly attracted to a particular activity: for example, a love for performing music, or for working with clay, or a love for being in a leadership role. When they do get in touch with their gifts, most people express them in very direct ways, such as:

I always knew I would be a teacher. I think I knew it by the time I was seven years old.

Or:

When I saw that everything in my life pointed to my interest in horticulture, something clicked for me. I saw all the way back to when I was five or six years old, when my aunt had me help her do her weeding. I loved the feeling of the dirt and the idea that you could plant a seed and it would turn into a beautiful flower.

Or:

I had always enjoyed hearing other people's stories and I knew that I was a good listener, that I could repeat their stories back to them and give them new ideas about their lives. When I saw how this was satisfied in my profession (marriage and family counselor), I saw a whole new side of counseling. I knew it was just right for me.

Usually when we are attracted to a specific activity, we also learn that we have a certain knack for it, and a desire to do that activity or to learn everything there is to learn about it. The attraction to the activity, the knack, and the desire to learn more can all be said to be expressions of the gift, coming from deep within us, indicating our innate skills and abilities.

WHEN OUR GIFTS ARE HIDDEN

For many people, the gift is obvious from the start. People who attain a high degree of recognition in their chosen professions, and who are happy doing what they do, frequently feel that they have always recognized their talent and have wanted to do that thing all their lives. But for others, the unique inner gift can be elusive indeed.

Often we are most blind to our own gifts, while being better able to see the gifts of other people in our work and in our relationships. One reason for this is that we are too close to our own gifts; they are the skills and attitudes with which we live every moment of our lives. We are, in effect, standing right inside it and so cannot clearly see our own gifts. There is a Sufi parable that makes this point in a rather colorful way.

The story goes that one day, in the greatest sea of all, two smaller fishes went to a large fish to ask his advice. "You are much older and wiser than us," the small fishes said. "We were wondering if you could help us."

The large fish, wanting to be helpful, replied: "Why, of course. I will do what I can."

"Well," the speaker for the smaller fish said, "we have been told that there is something called an ocean. It is filled with many mysteries and many interesting creatures. We would like to see this place. Can you tell us how to get there?"

The big fish felt like laughing, but not wanting to embarrass his younger counterparts—who, after all, had come to him seeking knowledge—maintained a serious face. "You are already in the ocean," he told them. "You are a part of it. The only way you can see it is to get out of it."

The same is true for many of us—that in order to recognize our gift, we must devise a way to "get out of it," to stand outside ourselves for a moment and look in, seeing our gift as others see it. This is particularly true when the gift is not clearly associated with a profession or career. For example, one can have a strong personality trait or a particular sensitivity, such as "a capacity to work with people and help them make use of their greatest abilities" or have "an eye for putting color together to create a sense of harmony" or "good organizational sense, with a particular talent for matching personalities to create work teams." These gifts may be extremely useful in any number of different life vocations. But in and of themselves, they are not vocations. We have to seek out those professions where these sensitivities can be applied, in a setting that meets other criteria of the Inner Self. Here's an example of how this might be done:

Beverly had a real eye for color and from an early age had enjoyed helping her friends choose their clothes. Because of her interest in color, she was advised by a school counselor to study fashion design. But Beverly quickly discovered that fashion design wasn't what she wanted. As she explored peak experiences in her life, she discovered that she also enjoyed, and was very good at, working with people. To make a long story short, she eventually decided that she wanted to be a personal fashion consultant. This meant that she would work with men and women for whom personal appearance was particularly important: executives of large companies, people in politics, entertainment, public relations, and so forth. She helped them choose their clothes, decorate their offices, and even pick out their cars. This career gave her the perfect opportunity for using and expressing both her "eye for color" and her ability to work with and enjoy other people.

I (Susan) think I was a typical example of a person who had difficulty seeing my own gifts and finding a way to make use of them in my work. My parents owned a resort when I was little. I grew up in the Sierra Nevadas, and in my child's mind I saw myself as an American Indian princess, always dressed in beautiful white buckskin. I always imagined myself growing up to one day be a very wise old woman. I do not know where I got this fantasy, but I suppose for a child who spent so much time alone in nature, it was a natural one to assume.

This self-image from my youth probably had a great deal to do with my early adult feelings of not "fitting in." After all, there are not too many professions that call for an Indian princess, all dressed in white buckskin! Though it might seem amusing in retrospect, I think many of our misunderstandings about our gifts may come from taking the symbols of our lives too literally.

Even as a very small child, I was most comfortable when I was simply sitting back and taking things in. I was a good observer and I was always intrigued by how things worked. *Process* intrigued me most of all, and watching an action unfold was very exciting to me. Most of all, I loved simplicity.

As far back as I can remember, I have planned out my steps. I like to figure out the simplest way to do things, whether it is a routine movement of my hand, a large business plan stretching over several years, or a vacation trip.

One of the things that I've always been aware of is that I have a clear sense of what it means to be in a human body. As a child, skiing was my main avenue of ecstasy.

It was my bliss. I would practice for hours until I had found the smoothest, most efficient path down a mountain. When I finally found that path, it was like a wonderful dance, almost like magic. Sometimes I would feel like a leaf floating on the air currents.

In many ways, my body is my world. I have always used my awareness to move around inside it, exploring how this area or that one feels, what's going on in there, how it works.

For many years, extending into my adulthood, I really wasn't very clear about my gifts. I hardly knew what they were. I just assumed that everybody did exactly what I was doing, that they were sensitive to the same things, and that they thought just as I did. Nevertheless, I used my gifts, even in the most routine jobs I had to do. For example, in the early part of my marriage I worked in an office at the University of California. Each morning I would look over what had to be done that day, and then I'd just sit quietly for a moment and plan the work out in my mind. I would look for the simplest way to do things, not because I was lazy, but because the simplicity pleased me and made the job enjoyable. A good day for me was when I could experience that simplicity in everything I did, whether it was answering the phone or typing or having a conference with my boss.

My formal education was in human development and special education. It seemed reasonable that these choices would make use of my special interests and gifts. What I saw, in working with people who were severely challenged physically, was that each truly was unique. I found that with my gifts, I could *go into a person's body* and get a sense of what each person was dealing with. With that knowledge I worked with them one to one, designing an educational or physical exercise program based on what I intuited about them. The problem was that in the classroom it was virtually impossible to make use of these gifts. Individual differences gave way to academics. There was little or no consideration for the fact that each person was unique. Touching was prohibited and there was no effort to connect on a personal level with people. The goal was to "mainstream," making no special demands on regular classroom teachers.

Each day we would set up the classroom, which meant strapping people into appliances that allowed them to be attentive to the teacher at the front of the room. Setting up would take fifteen to twenty minutes. There would then be fifteen or twenty minutes of teaching. The last fifteen or twenty minutes of the hour-long class would be spent taking students out of their appliances. There was a minimum of individual attention, and even these physically challenged people were "tracked" by "age-appropriate" scales, to measure scholastic achievement levels. The whole system was clearly aimed at making the student fit the teacher's mold, rather than having the teacher look at individual differences in order to find the most effective ways to meet student needs.

While still in school, I became interested in massage and bodywork. I was particularly drawn to systems that offered ways to look at individual needs, where there was attention given to each person's unique process. I found that these systems made use of my observational gifts and my longtime interests.

After studying the basic principles, I found myself attracted to body systems that emphasized simplicity as a path to healing. Through these systems, I saw that pain and discomfort were often the result of too much "efforting," that is, of not using our bodies in the most efficient or natural way. I loved using my observational gifts to go into people's bodies to try to understand these things. Then, healing nearly always occurred when I was able to work with these people to find the simplest, most efficient, and most effective way for them to use their musculoskeletal system in the activities that had been causing them trouble.

Numerous times during my bodywork career, I have been drawn back into the business world, thinking that it was the responsible thing to do, or that I needed to do it in order to have benefits, health insurance, to be paying into a retirement fund, or whatever. Each time I made these decisions, I knew they were against my own inner guidance. But out of fear or a concept of "doing the proper and accepted thing," I would do it. I never could quite get away with it. My Inner Self would protest, telling me I was on the wrong path. If I didn't pay attention to this message, I would become physically ill. Illness and physical problems would continue until I went back to doing my bodywork.

Over the years, my own system of bodywork has evolved slowly but surely, so that I now feel that I'm finally embracing my gifts and sharing them with others through my work. The work I now do involves a wonderfully simple two-step procedure: (1) observing the process by which clients use both their bodies and their minds to accomplish the things they do in their lives, and then (2) seeking the simplest, most direct, and most beautiful way for them to accomplish those things.

As Susan's story illustrates, a person's gift is often a very subtle thing. Sometimes it is found only by looking at a combination of skills and seemingly unrelated pleasures. So how do we learn about our own gifts? How do we identify them so that we can seek their clear expression? The best way to begin doing this is to experience the nature of the gift, first in other people—since we often can see others' gifts more clearly than we can see our own—and then in ourselves.

EXPERIENCING THE NATURE OF THE GIFT

Think of a close friend, a family member, or a loved one whom you particularly enjoy being with. Start focusing your attention on the talents or personal qualities that you most like about that person. Remember what we have discussed so far in this chapter, about the nature of our gifts and how they are less a matter of *what* we do than they are of *how* we do them.

As you turn your full attention to this friend or loved one, remember that our physical presence is part of the *self*, because it is partly through our physical bodies that we express what's going on inside us. When you are looking at physical qualities to find the gift, be particularly careful about looking at the ways the person holds his or her body, the way he or she moves—quick or slow, gracefully or clumsily, sensuously or mechanically, deliberately or casually, or any combination of these. All of these tell you something about the gift.

No two people look alike. It is almost as if our Creator has provided every single one of us with a unique exterior to remind us of the highly individualized gifts we each bring to the world with our lives. So when you admire a person's physical being, try to relate that to an inner quality the person has, a gift that is part of the Inner Self. For example, one woman described how she loved the way her boyfriend looked. He was, she said, "small and fluid" in his movements. When she looked further, to ask herself how these physical qualities related to an inner quality, or a gift that she loved in him, she said, "He has a comfortable way about himself that makes me feel comfortable about myself, and that way he has is kind of fluid and unobtrusive, the same as the way he moves."

By contrast, another person remarked how his best friend was tall, a little overweight, and even physically clumsy, but he found this attractive, if a bit comical at times. For him, all these qualities mirrored his friend's "outsized view of life, always a little ahead of himself, always anxious to jump into new territories, his ideas always bigger than life itself." Incidentally, this person was a gifted communications consultant who worked with large corporations and governmental agencies, helping to find solutions to interagency problems that often were, quite literally, bigger than life.

A third person spoke of her best friend from college, who was "a Mother Earth type, big-bosomed and with big feet always planted firmly on the ground." This woman said of her friend, "I always thought of her as this huge, sheltering oak tree." To her, the friend's physical solidity and substance mirrored an Inner Self that was completely comfortable with "the basics of life, like birth, death, and creating harmony in your living environments." With this gift, our proverbial "Mother Earth" eventually went on to raise five children, three of them adopted, on her own. As a single parent, she was also responsible for starting a community action hotline that kept a catalog of resources available to other single parents.

As you think about your friend or acquaintance's gift, don't limit yourself to the more obvious physical qualities, but look at qualities such as timing and rhythms. For example, Robert found that he loved being with his friend Judith because of the particular energy she exuded whenever she talked about things that interested her. He could not pinpoint any specific mannerism she had for expressing this energy.

To describe his friend's gift, as he saw her, Robert commented that "Judith is not particularly attractive in the classic sense, but whenever she enters the room, it is as if someone has turned on a brilliant and wonderful light."

When Robert told Judith these things, she could not at first take credit for them. Even though she knew that Robert enjoyed her company, she had never known that what he called her "energy" affected him, or anyone else, in this way. Her first response was "I don't know what he's talking about. I don't do anything but try to be myself." This notion of "being myself" is, no doubt, the key to discovering the qualities that make your Inner Self unique. Judith, by the way, was a dancer whose performances were particularly noteworthy because of her powerful stage presence, no doubt a product of those gifts that her friend Robert found so exciting about her.

Having explored the gifts of other people, you'll begin to develop a sense of what you're looking for. Now it's time to explore your own life in that way. How do you do this? Here is a list of questions to ask yourself that will help you get started:

- What do I most enjoy about myself?
- What is it that my friends most enjoy about me?
- When I am with other people, what is it that I feel is my contribution to the group?
- When I am alone, which of my personal qualities or capacities brings me the greatest pleasure?
- Think about your most highly developed skill, whatever it might be and regardless of how much more you feel you have to learn about it. Now ask yourself, "What is it in me that I want to express through this skill?"
- Think about any compliments people have paid you. For the moment, completely indulge yourself. Tell yourself, "Yes, I deserve that compliment. I really am _____." Fill in the blank according to what was said in the compliment. Bask in the compliment, even if you don't fully believe that it was deserved.
- If there was one personal quality or personal ability that you would not give up in your self, what would that be?
- If you would wish to be remembered for one thing after your death, what would that be?

As you go over this list, bear in mind that these are not questions we ordinarily ask ourselves. After all, you don't want other people to think you're immodest, do you?

If you are like most of us, you find that these questions aren't easy to answer. Your temptation may be to skip over this section, rationalizing that "Oh, I know what my gifts are. There's no need for me to go too much into that."

Take time to sit down with paper and pencil to describe your own gifts. (We'll be asking you to come back to this material when you get to the workbook section in the back of the book.) Some people find that the most important thing about this exercise is that they begin looking at qualities in themselves and others that seem to be expressions of their unique gifts. So we urge you to become familiar with the list of questions we've given above and remind yourself of them in the normal course of a day's activities.

In the days ahead, take note of these questions at those moments when you are particularly enjoying yourself. Quietly reflect on the gifts, skills, or attitudes that you brought to these moments, making them pleasurable for you.

When you are with friends, take note of any positive comments they make about you. Particularly notice the expressions on their faces when you are talking with them or touching them or working together on an activity that requires your joint cooperation. Ask yourself what you are doing that is satisfying to you while making a contribution.

At moments when you are alone, stop all activity and just take the time to appreciate yourself. Find one personal quality or gift that you particularly like about yourself, either one that you enjoy on your own or that other people seem to value. Let yourself be completely vain about this quality. Tell yourself how great you are, being mindful of the fact that this quality is one of your gifts.

Let yourself reminisce about one or more times when your gift helped you accomplish something that you deeply valued and enjoyed, or that had a positive effect on the people around you. Fully acknowledge to yourself that your gift played an important role.

Do your best at this time to turn off the inner censor who tells us that we shouldn't be vain. Remind yourself that the people who can most fully appreciate and value their own personal gifts are the ones who are most likely to make a contribution in this world. When we choose to remain blind to our gifts, they remain as invisible to others as they are to ourselves. But when we truly value them, we give of ourselves openly and generously, confident that by doing so, we can only gain.

MOVING FORWARD

In exploring your gifts in this chapter, you may have found that you had at least a certain amount of resistance about owning up to them. Most of us experience such resistance to one degree or another. Moreover, nearly all of us allow ourselves the luxury of seeing some of our gifts while staying blind or numb to others. Sometimes it is only minor gifts that we'll allow ourselves to take credit for, while remaining blind to the ones that are most important.

There is a specific reason that we find it difficult to own our greatest inner resources. They are often hidden from us by a self-imposed mask. This mask, which we created very early in our lives in response to painful interactions, confusions, or simply misunderstandings with the people around us, was originally used as a shield. It protects us from what Shakespeare once called "the slings and arrows of outrageous fortune," but at the same time that this mask protects us, it often hides our greatest gifts from us. And with our greatest gifts hidden in this way, we cannot make those unselfish contributions that finally allow us to feel that our lives are meaningful. This shield becomes so much a part of us that it often seems to be our "real" self.

Most of us go through life not even realizing that we

are wearing this mask. We become so familiar with how we feel when we are wearing it that we feel naked and vulnerable when we're without it. As you'll discover in the following chapter, when we look through the eyes of the Mask Self, our inner guidance is often confusing, leading us off the path. In lifting the mask, we find the gift beneath, from which our most positive and trustworthy guidance will come.

FIVE

Masks That Hide the Inner Self

"I can't explain *myself*, I'm afraid, sir," said Alice,
"because I'm not myself, you see."
"I don't see," said the Caterpillar.
—Lewis Carroll, *Alice's Adventures in Wonderland*

There is a teaching story from the Native American shamanic tradition that tells why the Inner Self is often hidden from us and how we can make sense of the messages
it sends us. In this story, the chief of the tribe has a son.
One day he goes to the boy and tells him that it is time
for him to take his first step into manhood. He tells him
that it is time to go on a vision quest.

The boy follows his father to the head of a trail that
starts at the foot of the mountains. He is instructed to go
to the mountains, to make himself a small camp on a particular ledge that faces the desert to the east. He shall
then fast for three days. The boy does as he is told. He
finds the ledge, high in the mountains, where others before

91

him have gone for the same purpose. He fasts for three days, and on the fourth night he has a dream.

The boy loses his way in the mountains. It begins to rain very hard. Because there is much lightning and thunder, he seeks refuge in a cave. The cave is dark, and as he enters, he hears a sound that frightens him. He feels something alive near him, reaches out, and is terrified to feel a hand grasping his wrist. He tries to pull away but cannot.

The boy struggles with a creature whose identity he does not even know. It seems to have many arms and legs, and he is certain that he will die. At last he finds his hands around the creature's throat, and with his last bit of strength he squeezes the windpipe closed. He feels the life go out of the creature, and when he is sure that it is dead, he himself tumbles away exhausted, and falls into a deep sleep.

In the morning, the sun coming in through the mouth of the cave awakens him. He remembers the fight with the creature from the night before, and he looks over to his left side, where the creature lies. He sees only the body of an old woman. He has killed a grandmother, a grandmother who is a shaman. The legends of his people had taught him that there was a shamaness of this description who lived in the mountains, with Bear and Coyote and Mountain Lion as her children.

He kneels over her, weeping. "Forgive me," he cries. "In the darkness I did not see who you were. I did not mean to kill you. It was the fault of the darkness. It made me fear for my life. Now I see what a terrible mistake I have made. What can I do to correct what I have done?"

The eyes of the grandmother flutter open. The boy watches as the leathery wrinkles of age, baked into deep creases by Father Sun, fade from her face. Soon her face is smooth, and he is looking into the eyes of a young man his own age.

"What is happening to me?" he asks. "Am I going

crazy? This is my own face I see, not the face of the grandmother."

The shaman speaks, answering him from the mouth of the young man. "You have only killed a part of yourself," the voice says. "You are still a child and have many things to learn. Do not blame the darkness for your error. Instead, look at your own fear. Your own fears are the cause. The lesson you have been given here is that your own fears are a mask, hiding the mysteries of your inner spirit from you. Last night you entered this dark cave and discovered your own powers for the first time. In the darkness of your ignorance, you recognized neither your powers nor your fears, nor did you know what you must do to claim them as your own."

"Does this mean that I will never have my power, that I will never be a man?" the boy asks, horrified.

"No," the grandmother who speaks with his own youthful lips says. "You will find your power, but first you must take off your mask of fear. You must come to know fear as well as you know the trails to the river where you have gone to bathe since you were born."

"But how shall I do that?" the boy asks.

"You must dare to show your man face to the world. That face is already within you. Only by being in the world as a man will you come to know your fears, and only then will the world come to know you as a man. This is the only path to your manhood."

"I don't know how to do what you have told me," the boy says. "Who will be my teacher?"

"Your own powers will teach you, just as they have done in this dream."

The boy awakens. He opens his eyes and sees that he is not in the cave, as he had thought. He is sitting on the ledge where he had made his camp four days before. He sees the small fire he'd made to keep himself warm. It has burned itself out, and now there is only a handful of cold, dry ashes.

He rises and goes back down the mountain. He finds his father waiting for him at the edge of the village. His father asks, "What have you learned from the mountain?"

"The mountain has taught me that it is now time to let the world see my man face," the boy replies with much pride.

His father begins to laugh.

"Why do you laugh?" the boy asks.

His father puts his right hand on the boy's shoulder. "You speak of it as a simple thing, like learning to build a fire," he says. "But showing your man face to the world is a journey that will never end."

"The grandmother in my dream told me that I would find this face beneath my mask of fear."

His father nods. "Yes," he says. "What the old woman told you is good. This knowledge is the first step of your journey. Now you cannot come back into the village as a boy."

The chief turns and begins walking back to the center of the village. But first he instructs his son to walk at his right side, the side of power.

HIDING THE POWERS OF THE INNER SELF

What we learn from this story is that those qualities which are the source of all our personal powers are often obscured from us by our own fears. Much of the time we cover our power with a mask which we have learned to wear as a way of protecting ourselves from the things we have been taught to fear. The mask itself causes us to look upon the world with fearful eyes, and eyes of fear always distort the truth, just as they did for the boy in the cave.

The trouble with the Mask Self is that its messages do seem to come from within. It is often difficult not to act on them, just as it was difficult for the boy in the cave not to act on them. Sometimes it almost seems as if the Mask

Self has the ability to cast a magic spell and disguise its perceptions or fear or anger as the *truth*. Much of the time our actions and the actions of the people around us are based on these false messages from the Mask Self. And this causes great confusion and hurt.

In essence, the Mask Self tells us to distrust our own inner guidance. It teaches us to look at the world through its eyes of fear and to look upon what happens in the external world as the cause of all our grief. It wants us to believe that the truth is always outside us. As long as we see the world through the eyes of our Mask Self, we will be convinced that we are completely at the mercy of what happens out there. Inner guidance isn't even in the Mask Self's vocabulary.

If lifting the mask is the way to discover our inner guidance, why can't we do it? One would think that having discovered these things, we would instantly tear off the mask and throw it away. But it is not that easy. As the shamanic story tells us, the act of accepting the power we possess in the Inner Self, and then bringing it forth into the world, takes a lifetime.

It is perhaps one of life's great ironies that our society does not generally teach us how to lift the mask of fear so that we can reveal our gifts and offer them to the world. So much of what we're taught in our early lives warns us to keep the mask in place, to distrust the guidance of the Inner Self, to put it aside in favor of what our parents, our peers, our teachers, our employers, and our society tell us.

If the shamanic tale with which we began this chapter presents these things on a metaphorical level, the following story, from a woman who attended one of our workshops, tells how the struggle to lift the mask and reveal the Inner Self works in real life.

BALANCING THE ACCOUNTS

Juliette was raised by parents who had suffered through several financial crises in their lives. They spent every waking hour thinking about money and how to get more of it. Juliette, on the other hand, was interested in art and design, and as a child, she spent many happy hours drawing and designing things. Her artwork was her bliss. Although she continued to express an interest in art throughout high school, her parents discouraged it, saying that there was no money in art and that if she chose it as a career, she would surely die in poverty.

There was so much pressure for her to study something more "practical and lucrative" than art that in the end, mostly to satisfy her parents, she went to a business school, where she studied accounting. Her parents were convinced that this was the best vocation for her, since accountants were always needed, and a good one could make a great deal of money.

Juliette, however, was not a good accountant. She didn't like working with numbers and had no interest in the work. At first she managed to earn a decent salary, but her heart was never in it and she eventually ended up making a serious error that got her fired. Dispirited and demoralized, she was convinced that she was a failure in life.

Looking back on it, Juliette reflected that everything she had done till then was done to satisfy her parents. The Inner Self, which was interested in art, was feeling frustrated and unrecognized.

Unable to face another accounting job, she applied for work with a temporary agency, where she requested an assignment as a receptionist. By chance, she was sent to work for a large ad agency. While she was there she visited the art department and was intrigued by the work that she saw people doing. It was like a dream come true for her. This was what she had been seeking all her life! This was where she could find work that would provide a way to express the longtime yearnings of her Inner Self.

Juliette continued working through the temp agency and began attending commercial art classes at night. Within four years she had opened her own graphic arts service, and two years after that she had already established a name for herself and was employing three other full-time workers. She reported that the energy and motivation she discovered after making the decision to commit herself to the skills and interests expressed through the Inner Self far exceeded anything she could have imagined.

LOVING AND PROTECTING THE INNER SELF

Life would be so much easier if the Inner Self staked out its claim from the first day we emerged from the womb, and thereafter continued to assert itself with a loud, clear, positive, and powerful voice. But we humans are complex creatures. Our training from infancy to adulthood is long. And in the process we are confronted with many frustrations that may cause us to distrust or be confused about these messages from the Inner Self.

If we were to create an ideal world, we would make certain that each and every baby ever born was welcomed into life by parents who were delighted by the presence of this new being in their world. In our fondest dreams we might wish for parents who just can't wait to embark on the wonderful adventure of discovering this new person's Inner Self and of watching the baby develop as an individual who has something quite new to offer the world. They would be bound to the child by feelings of unconditional caring and love, and by their own loving instincts to nurture and encourage all the new potentials that the baby can bring to life. They would encourage the child to move forward and grow, supporting that person's exploration of his or her own Inner Self as the key to education and movement toward maturity.

In this ideal world, all parents would have a profound understanding of the Inner Self as the individual's "homing device." They would know it as the source of their inner guidance and creativity, and they would be experts at helping their children learn to honor and trust that homing device. Every parent would be an expert at seeing the Inner Self, respecting and encouraging its growth.

As children, we would each grow up to know our Inner Self, and to know what we could and could not trust in it, because we had been tutored in following its guidance many times over in our daily lives, putting it to the test, getting to know it as one knows one's neighborhood or hometown. We would know the ecstasy of experiencing personal success through our own commitments to the beliefs and values of the Inner Self. And we would know the risks of personal failure and how to bounce back when our inner guidance didn't produce the results we felt we deserved.

But how many of us have had the good luck to enjoy such an ideal upbringing? And how many of us who are parents, even the most well-meaning parents, could ever completely live up to such lofty ideals!

Instead of being acknowledged and nurtured for our unique Inner Selves, most of us are born to parents who themselves have been frustrated in self-expression. After all, isn't it true that many of us grow up and move through our adult years without more than a vague awareness that the Inner Self exists? As people who have raised children, we know how difficult it is to nurture in our own children that which we don't recognize in ourselves. As parents, our reactions, for the most part automatic, are shadowed by many fears, most of them irrational:

"How can I ever satisfy this child's needs?"

"Will I be a good enough parent?"

"Will this child increase my burden?"

"Can I provide an adequate home, a college education?"

"Will I have to compete with this child for the affections of other family members?"

"How will this child affect other people in the family?"

Parents who have been disappointed in their efforts to
express their own Inner Selves may see in their children
an opportunity to fulfill their own frustrated aspirations.
They may see the child as the great dancer or athlete or
scientist they once thought they could be themselves.
Let's take a look at Irma, whose story illustrates how this
can work.

THE STORY OF A COMPASSIONATE
STAGE MOTHER

At twelve years of age, Irma was the rising star in a
popular ballet company run by a private school in the city
where she lived. At sixteen she toured the country and
enjoyed the applause of thousands of strangers, in cities
whose names she sometimes didn't even know. At sev-
enteen she signed on with a private touring company, and
by the time she was eighteen, she had begun using drugs.
A year later she stopped dancing, and at twenty, she entered a drug treatment program.

In the course of her treatment, Irma discovered that she
had never wanted to become a dancer. It became very
clear to her that while she enjoyed dancing, she hated
performing before a crowd. She was not afraid of performing. And for the most part, she enjoyed the attention she
got when she played to a large audience. But it was not

what "sparked" her. It was not what truly interested her. She had become a performer only to please her mother, who had always dreamed of a career on the stage. Irma herself wanted to become a schoolteacher, and a year after she graduated from her drug treatment program, she got admitted to college and happily began pursuing just that profession.

In Irma's case, she had a well-meaning mother who eventually acknowledged and came to respect her daughter's new choice. She even accepted responsibility for having pushed Irma toward fulfilling a goal that was actually the parent's goal, not the child's. Until Irma had found her own way, and had given herself permission to follow her own inner guidance and pursue a teaching career, she felt frustrated and resentful toward her mother. However, she had found it nearly impossible to express these negative feelings because her mother, after all, had "meant so well" and had believed that she only "wanted the best" for her daughter. The trouble was that "the best" for the parent was very different from "the best" for the child.

THE ESSENTIAL WOUND

The parents' inability to acknowledge and nurture the child's own unique inner nature forms what we call the Essential Wound. Frequently we are not fully open to the potentials of our Inner Self until we have healed this wound. Irma's Essential Wound was a belief that she would be valued and loved only for being a dancer, when her Inner Self was telling her to teach. As she healed the wound, she saw that she danced to satisfy her mother.

In Irma's case, her mother was able to let go of the selfish demands she'd pressed on her daughter, thus liberating Irma to begin exploring and following her own inner guidance. Unfortunately, few of us are lucky enough to have parents who are this insightful and emotionally generous. Most of us are destined to tackle the job alone.

THE MASK AS A SURVIVAL TACTIC

Along the way, we all learn a way of being in the world that is safe and acceptable to others around us. When we are very small, this safe and acceptable path appears to be a way to secure our basic necessities, such as food, shelter, and love. In many cases, this way of being provides a shield, the first hints of the Mask Self, that protects the vulnerable Inner Self hiding beneath it.

For the child growing up in a responsive, caring home, the Mask Self may consist of nothing more than becoming aware of common courtesies and learning to respect and honor other people's rights. In the ideal upbringing, there is plenty of opportunity to express the Inner Self so that both the Mask Self, with its focus on meeting outside needs, and the sources of our self-power are respected.

In some families, however, the Mask Self is valued above the Inner Self and its truths. As an extreme example of this, the child of an alcoholic mother may, for his or her own survival, have to learn how to anticipate the parent's moods, to give Mother what she wants in the hope of avoiding emotional or physical abuse. Note that the vulnerable Inner Self would be the recipient of that abuse. The child learns that by following his or her Inner Self, or by insisting that this self be heard, he or she may only make Mother angry, triggering her verbal or physical attack.

Through trial and error, or perhaps by following ancient survival instincts, the child constructs the Mask Self. He or she learns a way of being that keeps the mother at least partially happy some of the time. Having discovered that there is some correlation between the child's own behavior and how the mother treats him or her, the child feels he or she has at least some protection from the abuse that might otherwise have to be suffered. For the child, the

Mask Self quite literally becomes a necessary survival tool, a way to protect oneself and a way to minimize fears.

The Mask Self is nearly always a two-edged sword, inflicting as many wounds on the person who wields it as it inflicts on its adversaries. It may provide some protection from fear, abuse, or lack of security. And it may also provide some assurance that our basic needs will be met. But the child may come to feel that the Mask Self is so important that it eventually overshadows the Inner Self.

The peculiar thing about the Mask Self is that the more we act upon the illusions it creates, the more the world rushes in and appears to prove that the Mask Self's perception is true. We have all had experiences with this. For example, early in life we are taught that asking people for money is rude and that nobody will like us if we do it. From the perspective of the Mask Self, it really seems to us that whenever we need money, the world will look upon us in a negative way.

But let's say that the day comes when you want to borrow money to buy a new car. Through the eyes of the Mask Self the world becomes a fearful place. "People will reject you if you ask them for money," it seems to say. "Even if you go to a bank or to a loan company, you will be rejected." You feel this way even though you intellectually know that there are people who make a business of loaning money and that they would like nothing better than to sign you up for a loan. After all, you're a good risk and they know you will pay them a lot of interest over the next few years.

Nevertheless, because you see the world mainly through your Mask Self, you go around with a chip on your shoulder, convinced that no one is going to want to extend a loan to you. In fact, your Mask Self may be whispering to you, "Oh boy, nobody is going to like you now because you're out here asking people for money!" And sure enough, the first bank you go to turns you down. Your own self-doubts and fears have a way of being projected through the eyes of the Mask Self out onto the external world.

In ways that often can seem quite mysterious—though having a negative attitude when you ask for a loan just might have something to do with it!—we can actually create in the external world a reality that until this moment had existed only in our minds. And when we see our own self-fulfilling prophecies come true, through our own projections, we are more than ever convinced that the vision of the world that we see through the Mask Self is right. The Mask Self is always quick to play *I told you so* under these circumstances, saying, "Now maybe you'll pay attention to me when I try to warn you of these things. You see, I told you people would reject you and turn you down. Isn't this just proof of all I said?"

But, you might argue, isn't the Mask Self originally created out of signals received from the external world, that is, in reaction to the parent who can abuse, either in gross physical ways such as beatings, or in subtler emotional ways such as intimidation or put-downs? If we have learned these things directly from life, how can they be wrong or inaccurate? The point is this: The perceptions and the defenses the Mask Self learned may have been accurate and true for that particular situation, way back in childhood. But they do not necessarily continue to be accurate and true today. One very important aspect of the Mask Self is that it clings to the past, trying to convince us that whatever happened back then will happen again and again unless we continue to be on our guard every moment of our lives.

Sometimes even the most well-meaning parent can contribute to the creation of the child's Mask Self, through such things as overprotectiveness. Although overprotecting a child can be a selfish act on the part of the parent, it is seldom a vicious one. Through overprotectiveness, the child can adopt fears that exist only in the parent's mind. Most children are deeply sensitive to their parents'

fears. They become aware of the parents' emotional discomfort and they may begin looking around, trying to see
what it is that is so threatening. When the child can't find
anything to justify that fear, the child may begin to doubt
his or her own inner guidance. It is as though they are
saying to themselves, "My parents' perceptions must be
right and mine must be wrong." Of course, the real reason
the overprotected children can't see the threat is that the
danger perceived is completely in that parent's mind.

While the mask is in place, the person wearing it literally adopts the character it depicts. The person wearing
the mask might be compared to an actor who adopts the
character traits of his role. The Inner Self goes into hiding,
and the Mask Self leads the way. The experience we then
have is that we are completely ruled by events in the
external world, and nothing that inner guidance has to
offer is going to change that.

THE QUIET NICE GUY

There was a man we met in New York, whom we'll call
Joel, who told the story of how he had come to adopt a
Mask Self that he described as "the quiet nice guy." As a
child, he had learned to never make demands on his parents. They had both been alcoholics, and frequently when
he asked them for something, they grew angry with him
and went off on a tirade in which they sabotaged his character. Through their attacks he came to think of himself
as a selfish and demanding person who made his parents'
lives miserable. He came to see himself as responsible for
their drinking and their chronic unhappiness.

By trial and error, Joel found that their attacks on him
were minimized when he wore the mask of "the quiet nice
guy." He learned how to accommodate his parents, even
to the point of fixing meals for them, running errands, and
commiserating with them when they talked to him about

their troubles. He showered on them all the caring that he had wished for himself, and in giving this caring, he said, he found at least the illusion of satisfying those needs in himself.

None of this was a conscious choice on Joel's part. Like most children in his situation, he learned his behavior by responding to his self-indulgent parents' needs. It never occurred to him to act any other way since he did not have anything to compare his experiences to.

Joel had very low self-esteem as he grew up. In spite of all his efforts to please his parents, he was always, in his own mind, falling far short of his parents' standards. For many years, even in adulthood, he always spoke very highly of his parents. Moreover, he sharply criticized other people who expressed anything but positive feelings toward their parents. It was as though his Mask Self had to cling to the illusion that his parents were really very loving people whose lives would have been perfect had they been fortunate enough to be blessed with a more satisfactory child. Any guidance that he got from his Inner Self, telling him that he should follow his own instincts instead of always trying to satisfy his parents, was instantly rejected by the Mask Self.

In college he earned an M.B.A., and after his graduation he took a job as a manager with a large corporation. However, he found that he could not drop the quiet nice guy mask. He could never allow himself to make his needs known in his relationships at work or in his private life. He found it almost impossible to delegate authority or to reprimand employees who required discipline or guidance. People often took advantage of him, and in his zeal to accommodate others, he ended up taking on responsibilities that he could not possibly fulfill.

About a year after staring his new management position, he began displaying what his supervisor described as a bad temper. He would blow up over what seemed to be a minor thing while ignoring some of his employees' blatant violations of company policy, including such things as chronic tardiness and failing to meet production quotas.

Joel was referred to a management consultant, who pointed out to him the fact that he allowed problems to pile up rather than addressing them as they occurred. Worries and pressures then built up in his mind until he could no longer hold them. When he lost his temper and blew up, it was like a dam bursting, with all his frustrations spilling out helter-skelter, often directed at the wrong people or situations.

The consultant advised Joel to start paying attention to the small things as they came up throughout the day. If he did take care of these, he would not have to build up the dam of frustrations that led to his blowups.

As he looked closely at the quiet nice guy mask he always wore, he recognized that it hid a great deal of frustration and anger. Once he had identified what he needed in his life, he began seeking resources to help him learn new skills and to learn to honor his own needs and his own inner direction. Through a series of seminars, he learned to ask other people to assist him and he learned how to delegate authority. As he made these changes, he got more and more in touch with his Inner Self, a self that was really quite kind and caring but that also wanted, and eventually began getting, that same caring for himself in return.

Eventually he came to understand that the mask he wore as an adult was the same one he'd learned to wear as a child. One of his great revelations was that children are not supposed to be responsible for making their parents' lives okay for them. But this was the perception of life that he'd had as a child. As an adult, it was now possible for him to look back at his childhood and see that his negative self-image had been based on the false belief that his parents' unhappiness was the result of his inability to live up to their expectations. As he learned to trust his new knowledge, he was able to say no to the Mask Self when it tried to discount the messages from his Inner Self.

And in time he began to trust his own inner guidance, which liberated him from perceptions that he was always wrong.

THE MASK SELF IS NEVER SATISFIED

We see from Joel's story, and from others like him, that if the Mask Self is worn too long, or if it becomes the only way we can feel valued, we inevitably lose trust in our own inner guidance. Inner guidance becomes far more risky than following the direction that comes from the outside. Although we originally adopt the Mask Self for our own survival, we can actually lose our true identity through it. The Mask Self can become so familiar to us that we begin to believe that it *is* our true self.

The issue of self-esteem, which is such an important part of being a successful person in our relationships and in our work, has its roots in the Essential Wound and the Mask Self. Low self-esteem comes from not trusting one's own inner guidance. It comes from the Mask Self, which tells us that our own guidance is not important or worthy of consideration and that other people have answers that are better.

When the Mask Self dominates our lives, the Inner Self, ignored and unseen, becomes the source of a peculiar kind of pain. The Inner Self continues to seek expression and appreciation, but the absence of effective ways to express itself results in feelings of frustration, emotional pain, and emptiness. We often go into a spiral of mental activity around seeking but never finding what we're looking for. No matter how we may seek to satisfy the needs of the Mask Self, those feelings of emptiness will continue. The feelings of emptiness continue because the inner promptings that are crying out to be heard can only be satisfied by acknowledging the Inner Self and seeking to express it.

Thus, a person might choose the profession of engineering to satisfy the prompting of the Mask Self for a vocation that is "secure, clean, and financially rewarding." But this might be totally ignoring the Inner Self. One person we know chose the secure, clean, and financially rewarding way of life at the expense of satisfying his long-time love of music. He literally turned his back on his Inner Self.

In the beginning he felt that he had made a good choice. He enjoyed having money and a job where he could predict exactly what was going to happen the next day. But over time he began to feel bored and frustrated. Because the rewards of his job had initially excited him, he decided that the way out of his dilemma was to seek greater and greater financial rewards. He took on extra work, doing free-lance engineering in the evenings after his regular job. But the extra money didn't stop his feelings of frustration.

His feelings of emptiness continued since it was not the needs of the Mask Self but of the Inner Self that were crying out to be recognized and expressed. Ultimately his frustrations were quelled only when he began paying more attention to his own inner guidance. He began to look for a way to express what his Inner Self was seeking, that is, self-expression through music. This particular person continued his engineering work and satisfied the Inner Self through studying and playing music in his spare time. He made the choice to strike a balance between the needs of his Mask Self and those of his Inner Self.

RECOGNIZING AND HEALING OUR WOUNDS

Although the wounds that lead to the creation of the Mask Self can be crippling, they are seldom incurable. For example, adults who were sexually abused as children may require years of healing before they can truly enjoy physical intimacy with another person. But they *can* be healed.

The person who, as a child, is frustrated and injured (emotionally or physically) time and time again, when following the promptings of the Inner Self, or when trying to freely express the Inner Self and its unique truth, may become convinced that only in the Mask Self can safety be found. At its worst, this means living one's adulthood

PERSONAL CHARACTERISTICS
ASSOCIATED WITH THE MASK SELF

Emotion	Thoughts & Actions
Alienation, fear that "others won't like me."	Unsure where to fit in, seeking approval, drawn to other people who are in trouble or in need
Resentment	Distrust of intimacy & of "sharing"—things, ideas, personal achievements, or personal boundaries such as work or living spaces
Anger/hurt, low self-esteem	Feels he or she can only get needs met through manipulation or control of others
Shame/guilt	Looks to other people or external world for guidance and cues for what is expected of him or her
Distrust	Keeps to self, is watchful and defensive, rarely if ever shares feelings
Confusion when under pressure, bewildered by problems	Turns to external things such as drugs, exciting events, to make self feel better—may be "work addict," etc.
Loneliness, feelings of lack of support, need to be needed	Crisis-oriented life-style, or seeking troublesome, dangerous, or challenging relationships
Uncertainty about own ideas and feelings, numbness	Argumentative, sees things in black and white, unyielding when challenged, finds it difficult to see other's point of view

always seeking and responding to signals that come from the outside, and rarely giving voice to the Inner Self. One is literally at the beck and call of the external world and everyone in it, and so he or she may thoroughly lose touch with the Inner Self. In adulthood this person may feel completely lost unless there is some person or situation in his or her life to engage him in the proverbial "Dance of the Masks" that is most familiar and painful.

NEGATIVE MESSAGES FROM WITHIN

Most of the so-called negative emotions that we experience in our lives are the result of listening to the Mask Self and rejecting the guidance of the Inner Self. Destructive feelings, cruelty and even sadism, malice, jealousy, fear, anxiety, anger, hatred, and vindictiveness are all violent reactions to the frustration you feel when your own basic inner needs, emotions, and gifts are denied.

Following these negative promptings—that is, acting them out in the real world—invariably causes more problems than it settles. But certainly these are also inner promptings, ones that most of us feel very strongly from time to time. Aren't they part of this inner nature from which we take direction? They are, of course, but it is important to take a careful look at how these inner promptings work.

When the Inner Self is suppressed or frustrated over a period of time, fear, anger, and hatred can also be turned inward, where they are expressed in a variety of ways that have been mapped out by medical scientists. These include muscular tension, hormonal changes, changes in heart rates, respiration rates, and changes in blood flow. When these are prolonged, held in a physiologically abnormal state of tension by negative thoughts, they can disrupt the body's normal functioning patterns; they can do actual physical damage to the body. We get sick, sometimes in very obvious ways and sometimes in subtler ones. We are all aware of how stress, just one form of chronic frustration, can result in physical illness ranging from headaches and indigestion to heart attacks and cancer. Similarly, if the Inner Self is denied expression, the brain itself may begin to function in peculiar ways, causing mood shifts, or causing us to imagine offenses where there are none, even to the extent of making our personal relationships difficult or even impossible.

It is important to continually remind ourselves that it is through the Inner Self that we receive the ultimate source of all guidance in our lives. When we don't listen to it, or when we can't hear or understand the messages it sends us, we experience *dis-ease*. Dis-ease can come in the form of subtle, uncomfortable emotions, in the first stages, or in the form of full-blown medical problems, requiring professional assistance, in the later stages.

When we consider all these factors, it is easy to see why it is so important to acknowledge the Inner Self and to encourage its positive expression. When we are encouraged to allow this inner nature to guide our lives, we grow healthy, productive, and happy. When we continuously suppress it, we create dis-ease of the body as well as the mind.

No one would claim that it is always easy to make sense of the signals that seem to come from within. For example, one woman's fear prevented her from getting up and giving a speech that would help her secure a promotion in her career. She very much wanted the promotion and felt that she deserved it. But instead she chose to respond to the fear, that is, to the Mask Self. She made the decision not to give the speech.

We asked her if she felt that she was following the guidance of her Inner Self. There was not even the shadow of a doubt in her mind. She knew exactly what she had done. "No," she said, "I was not following my inner guidance. I allowed my fears to get in the way. That was an old program for me. I still feel like a little child who is supposed to be seen but not heard. In my heart I really wanted to stand up and be heard. I would have loved to follow this, but I just let old fears get in my way." She knew that she had suppressed her Inner Self rather than honoring it, and she later identified the fear she'd responded to as an expression of her Mask Self.

Negative emotions—anger or sadness or ambivalence or self-criticism—following a decision like that described in the preceding paragraphs always tip us off to the fact that we did not follow the guidance of our Inner Selves. If we had followed it, we would feel inner peace or perhaps we'd even celebrate our decision. We learn how to listen for the subtler signals of the Inner Self, and to separate those messages from the ones sent by the Mask Self, only after we deepen our self-understanding and discover the ways we have of throwing barriers into our own paths. That deepening of understanding begins by looking at how conflicts and misunderstandings in our early lives affect the Inner Self.

REBIRTHING THE INNER SELF

Fortunately for us all, the Inner Self never dies. We certainly can box it in and drive it into hiding, obscuring it behind the Mask Self and its machinations. But the Inner Self can be awakened and given new life at virtually any time.

Literature abounds with statements about this transitional period in one's life, of moving toward self-empowerment, away from taking our direction from pressures or influences outside us and toward taking direction from our Inner Self. One of our favorite quotes along these lines is from Ralph Waldo Emerson's essay on "Self-Reliance":

There is a time in every man's education when he arrives at the conviction that envy is ignorance; that imitation is suicide; that he must take himself for better, for worse, as his portion; that though the wide universe is full of good, no kernel or nourishing corn can come to him but through his toil bestowed on that plot of ground which is given him to till. The power which resides in him is new in nature, and none but he knows what that is which he can do, nor does he know, until he has tried.

This single paragraph describes the goals of this book better, perhaps, than any we have yet found.

EXPERIENTIAL EXERCISE: RECOGNIZING THE INVOLVEMENT OF YOUR MASK SELF AND INNER SELF IN YOUR LIFE

Purpose: The purpose of this exercise is to start you thinking in terms of your Mask Self and Inner Self, and how they affect your trust in your inner guidance. It is designed to help you get in touch with how the Inner Self and Mask Self actually feel to you. As you follow the instructions, bear in mind that most activities in our lives involve both the Mask Self and Inner Self. Ideally, we feel most satisfied with ourselves when there is at least a balance between the two.

Instructions: Think about an activity in your life that you particularly enjoy doing on a fairly regular basis. This can be anything from sitting at home reading a book to working with large groups of people in a public setting. Imagine yourself engaged in this activity. See and feel yourself doing what you do, totally involved in the pleasure of it.

What is the dominant emotion you experience? Is it a feeling of relaxation and peace or is it a feeling of high excitement and stimulation? Is it a combination of these? Or is it some other feeling, such as a sense of victory, or a sense of being "at one" with everything around you? Is it a sense of deep accomplishment, or is it a sense of being in harmony with the thoughts and feelings of another person? Whatever you are feeling as you remember yourself engaged in the activity you love, try to put words to it. Here are some examples:

> I love backpacking in the mountains, knowing I am at least ten or fifteen miles from the nearest civilization. I get a tremendous feeling of knowing that I am part of the natural order of things. I know that my survival and comfort are based on my own actions in the here and now. All the complexities of my job and my life in the city get washed away, and I get what is really important in my life back into perspective.

Or:

> I love to cook. Sometimes I completely lose myself in what I'm doing, and there is the sense that everything is just unfolding on its own, like a flower blooming in one of those ultraslow-motion films. I would say that I feel very calm and centered, not having any sense of even having to think about what I'm doing. . . . It's just a wonderful sort of effortlessness.

Now consider the following questions:

1. When you first get involved in this activity, what is it that gets you interested?

2. While you are engaged in this activity, how do you relate to the people around you?

3. Was there any preparation involved? If so, how would you describe that preparation?

4. Was there the presence, or perhaps an obvious absence, of a challenge or conflict to overcome? If so, how would you describe it?

5. Did you feel a deep sense of commitment any-where along the way, or was there a sense of noncom-mitment?

6. Was organization involved? If so, what part did you play in it?

7. What was the payoff or reward, if any?

8. How did you end the experience?

9. How did you feel after completing this activity?

10. Did you have any thoughts about how other peo-ple might be affected by this experience after you had completed it? If so, describe.

Here is how one person answered:

When I took up bicycling ten years ago, the thing that got me interested was that my friend had just purchased a beautiful touring bike. That summer he rode across the U.S. with a group, and I was tremendously jealous. At first I felt that a ride like that was totally out of my realm, but I'm a competitive person and I had to try. I went out and researched the thing, the kind of bike to get, training pro-grams, everything, and then I was just launched into it. I was hooked! The first few months were punishment, as I got into condition, and then it got easier and easier until I felt that I could do anything. I didn't get into touring, though. I got into racing instead, and have now qualified in two races. I haven't won any prizes yet, but I'm keeping up with the pack and I'm proud that my performance is at least competitive. It's really a great feeling to be out there like that.

While most experiences in our lives involve both the Mask Self and the Inner Self, it is usually the Mask Self that seeks approval from people outside you, or that looks to them as a measure of your own self-worth. It is, for example, expressed in the competitive spirit in the bike rider's story above. When the Inner Self is engaged or being expressed, your satisfaction comes from deep within you and appears not to depend on feedback from the external world.

Without being too analytical about it, look over any notes, or consider any thoughts you had while doing this exercise. Ask yourself which parts of the experience engaged the Mask Self and which parts engaged the Inner Self.

EXAMPLE

Dennis was a marathon runner and got a great deal of pleasure from competing in organized runs. As he looked carefully at his activity, following the above instructions, he found that he had originally gotten into organized sports as a child. He had joined a Little League team in order to win the approval of his father, who had always dreamed of having a professional career in baseball. Although Dennis's fondest memories of his father were involved with his Little League activity, he knew it was not something he would have chosen to do on his own. So he decided that this part of his involvement in organized athletic activities came from his Mask Self.

On the other hand, during a long run, he found that he always got into a state of deep concentration when he felt totally in touch with his body. At these times, he seemed filled with self-confidence (even when he wasn't winning the race), and he found that really wonderful solutions to problems at work or in his personal life simply flowed to the surface. He always felt that he could get an answer to any problem by going out for a long run. He decided that this level of involvement had to be associated with his Inner Self.

This exercise is strictly for your own information, so that you may begin to think about how the Mask Self and Inner Self work in your life. By simply becoming aware of the thoughts and feelings associated with these two important parts of yourself, you gain the ability to make the choices necessary for following your bliss.

MOVING FORWARD

In this chapter we've explored how the Mask Self affects our trust in our own inner guidance and how it often obscures the messages from our Inner Selves. Knowing how the Mask Self inhibits us is important, of course. But what is even more important is knowing how to lift the mask so that we can reveal the Inner Self and begin to trust it more.

We already know that the mask is the result of learning to distrust the guidance of the Inner Self. Now we need to explore how we can lift the mask by addressing the Essential Wound that caused us to create it in the first place. Although the inner "pep talk" of positive affirmations and creative visualization can nudge us in the direction of trusting our inner guidance more, it is only by going to the root of the problem that we can experience long-term success. The root of the problem, in the case of the Mask Self, is the experience that we call the Essential Wound. In the following chapter we describe simple but direct ways to locate those wounds in our own lives and begin to heal them.

SIX

Healing the Essential Wounds

Full wise is he who knows himself.
—Geoffrey Chaucer

"My parents were really very loving people," Mary told the twenty-three people who, like her, were sharing stories of early wounds in their childhoods. "But I think they were overprotective of me. I have always loved animals, and I still do even today, but they had all kinds of reasons why I shouldn't have pets."

Mary, a trim, attractive woman in her early thirties, sat telling her story to the workshop group. She was the model of reserve and propriety, both feet planted firmly on the floor, hands folded neatly in her lap. She was polite and pretty, her voice as soft as a child's. She wore a bright, flowery summer dress with a lace-trimmed bodice and collar.

We had just asked the group to think about events in their pasts when their own inner guidance had come under question. This assignment would help them identify the Essential Wound, which was at the root of their distrust of their Inner Selves. We had explained that this wound was often found in experiences of having one's ideas or opinions belittled, ridiculed, or in some cases, simply proven unworkable. And sometimes it arose when a traumatic event occurred while acting on one's own guidance.

For most of us, the Essential Wound is not one wound, but many. For some people it may even be many smaller events leading up to one. For others, there may be a single event upon which they focus as their Essential Wound, although there may have been many smaller ones along the way.

Although we have always referred to it as the Essential Wound, several people in our workshops have suggested another word: the "Essential Misunderstanding." As you read on, you'll better understand why this is, and you might also prefer to use this second term.

To identify their own Essential Wounds, we ask people to think about times in their lives when they are going along, doing something that completely delights them, feeling completely confident and at one with themselves. Then something changes abruptly. Perhaps, if they were a child at the time, an adult came in and punished them. Or someone laughed at them. Or someone got hurt.

The common denominator in all of these Essential Wound experiences is that they are moments in our lives when we begin to realize (consciously or unconsciously) that there is a difference between our perceptions of the external world and the world itself. Such experiences can indeed be very disturbing. When we have experiences that call our perceptions into question, they point out to us that what our senses seem to be telling us is not always true. These moments make us realize that if there is a line of communication between our senses and the external world, it is not a direct one. Somewhere along the way we assign meanings to the messages coming into our brains from our senses, meanings that distort the truth. We thus end up attributing qualities to the external world that in reality are products of our own perceptions. Alfred North Whitehead, the American mathematician and philosopher, once commented on this point:

> The poets are entirely mistaken. They should address their lyrics to themselves, and should turn them into odes of self-congratulation on the excellency of the human mind. Nature is a dull affair, soundless, scentless, colorless; merely the hurrying of material, endlessly, meaninglessly.

These Essential Wounds are universal. On one hand they initiate us into what it means to be human. After this initiation, we begin to struggle, consciously or unconsciously, with the realization that we ourselves are responsible for the perceptions that determine our life paths. On the other hand, these wounds help us identify key events that have made our Mask Selves what they are.

Mary continued with her story: "My parents were missionary workers, and when I was quite small, we lived in India. Our house was in a kind of suburban area, but just outside our back door was what I guess you'd call a jungle. I was about four years old at the time, and quite precocious. I remember that every afternoon it got very hot and everyone took a siesta, like they do in Mexico. Well, while everyone was asleep I decided to go on a little adventure by myself.

"I knew about this path that went out behind our house into the jungle, and I was walking along it when I saw a snake. It was a large cobra, maybe five or six feet long, but I wasn't the least bit afraid of it. In fact, I really liked the snake, and as it slithered along the path, I decided it was my friend and a pet, and I began playing with it. I remember actually petting it, and then I walked along with it, talking to it and sort of straddling it, with one leg on each side of its body as we went along.

"I was really enjoying myself, and even today I am convinced that the snake and I understood each other. We were friends and playmates, and we never would have hurt each other." Mary paused, tried to speak, but choked up. In a moment she was sobbing, tears rolling down her cheeks. The woman sitting next to her held Mary for a moment, consoling her, and after a few minutes she regained her composure enough to tell us the rest of her story.

"The snake and I went quite a ways into the jungle together, along the path. I don't know how far we went. It seemed like quite a ways. Then we came upon some men, and when they saw me they suddenly started shouting, and one of them rushed in and pulled me aside. As I watched, two other men drew machetes and chopped the snake to bits, right in front of me."

Mary, the child, had been horrified and inconsolable. Her perception had been that the snake was her friend, her pet, and they had a common bond. There was love between them which she believed they both understood and honored. In her mind she was convinced that she was safe, and certainly she was happy in her *pet's* company. Then, abruptly, they came upon a group of people who did not share that reality. To the men with the machetes, the reptile was a dangerous enemy which could turn on them and with a single blow inject its deadly venom. And so they had felt compelled to destroy it.

The story could have played out another way, of course. What, for example, would have happened if Mary had tripped and fallen on the snake? Would the cobra have interpreted this as an attack and turned on her, delivering its deadly venom in its own defense? We can't possibly know that, and of course, Mary would probably not have been around to tell her story had it happened that way. But in either case, this was an excellent example of an Essential Wound, a moment in Mary's life when she discovered that the rest of the world did not share her own inner reality.

But of what significance is this knowledge about the Essential Wound? How can it be applied in our lives, and what does it have to do with following our bliss?

As Mary worked with her story about the snake, she began to put together a picture of her Mask Self. She told us that she had had a secret desire, all her life, to become a veterinarian. She loved animals and wanted to work with them. When she thought about doing this, she felt calm, focused, delighted with herself. To be a veterinarian was her bliss.

"What has stopped you?" we asked.

"That my parents never approved," she answered. "And..."

"And what?" we asked her.

"I don't know. The dream is just perfect for a while. In my mind I see myself doing my work with animals and loving how I feel. Then something changes. I just have this sense of—I guess I can't describe it any other way—this sense of impending doom."

One of the other participants in the class asked her, "Is it like what happened to you when the men killed the snake?"

Almost immediately, tears welled up in Mary's eyes and she began to weep. She had struck upon the truth of her Essential Wound. All her life she had pushed back her own inner guidance. All her life she had distrusted her desire to become a veterinarian and work with animals. Her distrust had come from the Mask Self, which was her mind still trying to protect her from the horror of her experience in the jungle that day.

As she left us after the workshop, Mary said that she felt much clearer about trusting her inner guidance now. She was no longer confused by the fear that arose from the Mask Self whenever she entertained her dream. She said that she was going to start exploring ways that she might go back to school and study veterinary medicine. She was certain that this was what she wanted to do with her life. This was her bliss, and she felt that confronting her Essential Wound had helped her stop doubting herself.

Although we lost touch with Mary after the workshop, and so can't report whether she followed her bliss or not, her story does offer a good example of how healing the Essential Wound can help us gain freedom from our Mask Selves and increase our trust in our inner guidance.

FALSE TRUST IN THE MASK SELF

It is important to see that we each do possess an inner reality, which is not exactly like the inner reality of anyone else in the world. Although not necessarily leading to dramatic confrontations, as in the story Mary told, the fact that we each perceive the world a little differently does present us with the potential for conflict, disappointment, insecurity, frustration—all of those and more.

When we are very small children, our sense of security, our sense that it is okay to be in the world, is precariously balanced. We need to feel that our inner reality is, for the most part, trustworthy. We need to be able to act upon what we perceive and be at least somewhat assured that our actions will be appropriate and rewarding. When it turns out that our perceptions aren't completely trustworthy, as will occasionally happen, we need to feel that we can fall back on the judgment of a more experienced person. There's an added consideration which is even more important here: As children, we are dependent on our parents for providing certain basic needs—food and water, hygiene and caring, protection and affection. Even the tiniest infant recognizes this at a deep, visceral level.

To feel safe as children, we must create, as part of our inner reality, a perception of the parent as trustworthy and loving. And rest assured, our minds are very creative when it comes to doing this. We are all very capable of creating illusions of security and trust that completely overrate our parents. In some cases, the child's need to make the parent okay is so great that his or her illusions could better be described as lies, lies that put the child in danger of further injury.

I (Hal) recall the story of a four-year-old girl at a Head Start program where I taught my first year after college. This beautiful little child came into nursery school one morning with her hands crudely bandaged. Upon closer inspection, the head teacher under whom I worked discovered that both hands were horribly burned and there were signs that infection had set in. The school contacted the parents and rushed the child to the hospital for emergency treatment of what turned out to be third-degree burns with the complication of infection.

The child's father was questioned by social workers, and he confessed to them that he had held her hands on a hot stove to punish her for something she'd done. On the day after this happened, the head teacher of the child-care center was visiting the child at the hospital. The little girl's hands were still bandaged with gauze, so that it looked like she was wearing white boxing gloves.

As the teacher talked with her, the child suddenly pulled herself up on the side of the crib, and with arms outstretched and a bright smile on her face, she delightedly called out, "Daddy!" The father, who had come to visit her, ran over to the crib and picked her up. The little girl hugged her father and excitedly told him about the ice cream the nurses had given her and pointed to the little stuffed toy the teacher had brought her—relating all the things that children frequently share with their parents. As far as the teacher could see, the child was being very spontaneous, and was genuinely happy to have her father at her bedside.

The point we wish to make here is that the child's love and need for her father made her blind to the fact that he had brutally injured her. Deep in her mind, the child had made her father okay. Certainly other people recognized that the father was not trustworthy. But the child seemed to be oblivious to this. She had created a Mask Self that blinded her and made her distrust her Inner Self and turn away from her own inner guidance.

As adults, most of us have had the experience of "blind love," of being infatuated with a person whose behavior was damaging or hurtful to us at some level. In our minds, we either blind ourselves to that negative behavior or, like the burned child, we manage to figure out a way to make that behavior okay.

Until we learn to trust our own inner guidance and see the other person's weaknesses and strengths with some degree of clarity, we aren't being loving or caring. We are only playing out a shared script that may finally prove to be frustrating and destructive for us as well as the other person.

BLAME AND FORGIVENESS

Many of us struggle for years, if not our whole lives, with the puzzles growing out of our own Essential Wounds. One of the most common ways we do this is through blame; we blame the person (usually a parent) who we feel inflicted the wound. Or we blame ourselves for some act that we may feel caused the wound. Very early in our lives, we seem to adopt the belief that if we can only find a place to attach blame for our wounds and discomforts, we will somehow be okay. But nothing could be further from the truth. When we blame, we continue to hold on to the wound. The blame keeps us in a kind of limbo, constantly focused on our Essential Wound or burying it deep in our unconscious minds, with a thick overlay of rationalization and confusion. However we do it, blaming has a way of keeping us looking at the world only through the eyes of our Mask Self. This blame prevents us from seeing what we can do to heal the wound and begin taking responsibility for our own lives.

In my own life, I (Susan) clearly remember the first time I confronted my own blame. I had just been divorced and was a very young woman with three children to raise. I felt terribly frightened and angry, and I directed most of my anger at my mother. Somehow I saw her as the cause of all my present grievances.

Then something happened to change how I looked at this. I'm not sure how it came about, but I had a revelation that absolutely convinced me that my parents really had done their best in raising me. They had loved and cared for me, and I knew, being a parent myself, that this is the most that we can do. Knowing that my parents had done their very best, I also began to see the absolute futility of blaming anyone—including myself. I realized that regardless of what had happened in the past, my life was my own; only by letting go of my blame could I ever learn to trust my inner guidance and get on with my life.

DARING TO PEEK UNDER THE MASK

In exploring what it means to fully accept our own humanness, the author Sheldon Kopp once wrote:

> God tugs at the pilgrim's sleeve telling him to remember that he is only human. Each man is capable of warmth, of loving, of extending himself, of being transparent and vulnerable to another. At the same time, and perhaps in the same proportion, he is capable of evil, sham, fraud, and destructiveness, of closing out the other and wantonly using him.

We are most successful at healing our own wounds when we recognize that any one of us is capable of being both victim and victimizer. We are capable of being hurt and we are also capable of hurting other people, and to heal one, we must be able to accept that both deserve to be healed. This does not mean that "anything goes," or that we have to ignore or condone injurious acts. On the contrary, healing begins when we allow ourselves to fully acknowledge that the hurtful or destructive action has occurred. But holding on to the blame neither heals the wound from which we suffer nor protects us from further harm. In fact, holding on to blame is just another way to hold the mask in place. We continue to see the world through the eyes of the Mask Self for as long as it's there, and *the lenses of those eyes continue to warp the world we see.* As long as we see the world through that warp, nearly every new experience we encounter holds the potential for being a repeat performance of the Essential Wound.

In this book we have one goal where healing the Essential Wound is concerned: It is to regain trust in our own inner guidance, giving us the renewed ability to follow our bliss. With that in mind, let's take a look at how we might go about our healing.

LETTING GO OF OUR BLAME

Most Essential Wounds have three common characteristics. When we're familiar with these, healing can begin, the doubts and fears of the Mask Self are minimized, and we find ourselves gaining trust in our own inner guidance. These are the common characteristics:

1. **They are based on limited knowledge.** At the time that we suffer our first Essential Wounds, we are only beginners in life. We have an incomplete picture of what really happened and why. The most perplexing puzzle we face at this time is the need to see our parents as ultimate authorities, bigger than life, all-seeing and all-knowing. We learn true forgiveness and release ourselves from the

closed circle of blame only when we are finally able to free our parents to be mere mortals like ourselves.

One important result of the limited knowledge we have in our early years is that we tend to see the wound as having come about as the direct result of something we did, or something that someone else did. It is an illusion that there is a direct cause and effect. We are blind to an important step that lies in between, which is the involvement of our own perceptions and the perceptions of others. For example, part of Mary's wound was a question about her own guilt for what she believed she had done to cause the snake to be destroyed. In other words, she believed that she did something wrong which caused the snake to be killed. A more complete picture would have included the realization that the workmen's *perceptions* of the snake as dangerous caused them to destroy it. And no matter what we might like to believe to the contrary, we cannot be responsible for other people's perceptions; we can only be responsible for our own.

To be released from her own feelings of guilt, and to stop the endless cycle of looking for others to blame, Mary had only to see that everyone involved did the very best they knew how to do at that moment, based on their own perceptions of what was happening.

Similarly, in the example we gave in the previous chapter on the Mask Self, Joel adopted the mask of "the quiet nice guy" because he believed that he was responsible for his parents' unhappiness and could make them happy by adopting this role. Only much later in his life did he see that their perceptions of their lives, not his behavior, caused them to feel as they did. They projected their dissatisfactions about their own lives onto him.

2. They include our own illusions about our parents. At the time these wounds occur, we are dependent on our parents for love, protection, support, and the basic necessities of life. We desperately need the people we're dependent on to be trustworthy and right, even when there is evidence to the contrary. In an unconscious effort to maintain this illusion, we may go so far as to blind ourselves to the truth about them.

In Mary's case, her perception of her parents as kind and loving people was accurate. What's missing from this picture is that their perceptions that pets are a waste of time was not an ultimate truth, not completely trustworthy. Their perceptions came from their own very religious upbringing, by strict Fundamentalist parents, people who were convinced that expressing affection for animals was practically a sin.

The interesting thing to note here is that as long as she tried to maintain her illusion that her parents should be authorities in all things, Mary continued to be caught up in an impossible tug-of-war between her parents' antipet beliefs and her own inner guidance that animals are wonderful creatures worthy of her love, trust, and care. As she let go of her illusions that her safety and happiness depended on her parents being ultimate authorities, she also gained trust in her own inner guidance. She saw the way clear to follow her bliss.

3. Unhealed wounds produce feelings of blame. Until Essential Wounds are healed, we tend to seek blame, in others or in ourselves, for any difficulties we are having in our lives. In reality, blame may be nothing more than our unconscious effort to create a sense of certainty, to find an explanation for a painful experience. It is almost as if our Mask Selves are saying: "If I can attach blame to someone or something, I will know how to avoid it in the future. Then I can keep up my guard against this horrible thing and have assurances that it won't happen again."

Whatever we may believe we are accomplishing with blame, one thing is certain: As long as we hold on to it, it keeps our Mask Self in place, preventing us from being able to trust our own inner guidance. It keeps us focused

on the past rather than allowing us to be flexible, responsive, and open to the present. When we are finally able
to let go of blame, we are released from the Mask Self
and we can then become increasingly more comfortable
with the present and our inner guidance. We can break
through into the light, where we can follow our bliss.

In the beginning, Mary felt that she had to make a
choice between her parents' beliefs and her own inner
guidance. She blamed them for being imperfect. Whenever she decided to trust her own guidance, she felt she
was being disloyal to her parents. She felt terrible when
this happened. She stopped the vicious circle of blame
and confusion only when she saw that both she and her
parents had a right to their own separate and different
perceptions.

If all this sounds complicated, bear with us; the healing
is much easier than you might think.

THE HEALING

Probably one of the most difficult things to see and
accept is that in our adulthood, the Essential Wound is
our own perception—not something that exists in the external world. Although we were probably not solely responsible for choosing it or creating it in the beginning,
we are now solely responsible for re-creating it moment
by moment, every second of our lives.

This does not mean that we re-create it consciously and
deliberately, or that we choose it the same way we might
sit down one day and choose to buy a new car or a television set. But we do continue to hold these wounds within
our own minds. We maintain these perceptions, and as we
do so, they tend to serve as models for our own behavior.

One of the first steps we can take to heal the Essential
Wound is to create what we call the Self Advocate. The
purpose of the Self Advocate is to remind us that each

and every one of us has a right to our own inner reality. The Self Advocate helps us broaden our perceptions of those events that led up to the Essential Wound. Creating the Self Advocate allows us to liberate ourselves from blame, heal the Essential Wound, and rediscover how to trust our own inner guidance.

CREATING THE SELF ADVOCATE

For a moment, imagine that you have a best friend who is completely supportive of you. This friend has the deepest respect and love for your beliefs and feelings. He or she knows you through and through, and above all, is completely accepting of the fact that you have an inner reality that is different from anyone else's in the world. In fact, this friend has the theory that each and every one of us has been given a different inner reality for a definite purpose. Nobody knows what this purpose is, but it is this friend's mission in life to remind us all that our own and everyone else's inner reality should be respected and supported. This is your Self Advocate.

Now let yourself go back to that event that you have identified as your Essential Wound. Everything is the same except that this time your Self Advocate is there by your side. As an example of how this might work, let's return to Mary and her love of animals.

Mary is having an argument with her parents. She is telling them how much she wants a pet, and they are telling her that she can't have one. She is in tears. She feels hurt and humiliated and bewildered as they tell her that we should not give in to the temptation to develop emotional attachments to animals.

At this point, Mary's Self Advocate steps in and says: "Mary, I want to remind you that you have a complete right to your own inner reality, which is your love of animals." Then she imagines her Self Advocate turning to her parents and telling them: "You have a right to your inner reality, too."

Speaking to both Mary and her parents, the Self Advocate asks: "What can we do to make certain, right now, that everyone's inner reality is respected? To do this, we have only to give each other the same rights we would ask for ourselves. Right now, Mary needs support in her inner reality."

Mary now imagines that her Self Advocate turns to her parents and asks them to tell her something. A moment later, the parents tell Mary: "We love you and want to support your inner reality. We believe that it is important and good, and we encourage you to lead your life with this as your guiding light. For now, we still do not want animals in the house, but that is only because of our own beliefs. We do not want you to misunderstand why we are doing this. Your inner reality is important, but so is ours, and for the moment we simply don't know how to change."

Mary's Self Advocate now turns to her and tells her: "Now you are an adult. Many things have changed since this experience of the Essential Wound. The most important thing for you to look at now is that you no longer have to make a choice between your inner guidance and your parents' beliefs. When you were a child, you felt that you needed to make your reality match theirs. You depended on them for love, protection, and the basic necessities of life. You needed to believe they were right. But now you provide these basic necessities for yourself, and you are completely free to fully honor your own inner guidance. You need no longer feel that you are caught up in the old game of tug-of-war between your inner guidance and your parents' beliefs."

All of this is, of course, an inner dialogue designed to communicate with your Inner Self. Communication with your Inner Self is most effective, producing the longest-lasting results, when it is loving and nonjudgmental. Notice that in these imaginary conversations with the Self

Advocate, there are no adversaries; the Self Advocate asks for and gets support not by choosing sides, but by affording the same rights to everyone concerned.

Here are some steps to follow for simplifying this process.

1. Imagine having a friend, the Self Advocate, who is completely supportive of you. This friend has the deepest respect for your inner reality, your beliefs, and your feelings. He or she also firmly believes that each and every person has been given this separate inner reality for a larger purpose, which we can perhaps never know. Your Self Advocate believes that it is very important to learn this and to learn how to honor and protect this inner reality in each and every person, including yourself.

2. You imagine your Self Advocate telling you the following: "You have a complete right to your own inner reality." You can elaborate on this in any way you wish, defining what that reality is, saying something about how you will develop that inner reality even further, etc.

3. Allow yourself to go back in time to a particularly vivid memory of an Essential Wound in your life. Now imagine the Self Advocate addressing every person involved, telling them: "Each and every person here has a right to his or her own inner reality." If you wish, let the Self Advocate explain everything described in paragraph 1.

4. The Self Advocate now goes around to each person, reviewing whether or not his or her inner reality is being recognized and respected by the others. If it is not, the advocate asks those who are not supporting that person to do so.

Notice that the Self Advocate never asks anyone to give up his or her own inner reality or even to change it. He or she simply insists that no one undermines anyone else.

5. The last step is to have your Self Advocate remind you that you are now an adult. You no longer have to choose between your own inner guidance and your parents' (or others') beliefs. You are no longer dependent on these people for love, protection, and the basic necessities of life. You can now secure these for yourself. You are completely free to honor your own inner guidance and be true to yourself. The old tug-of-war between your parents' beliefs and your own inner guidance is gone.

When working with the Self Advocate in the way described in the preceding section, some people seem to have to wrestle with their own resistance. They might find themselves arguing, "But my dad would never listen to someone who talked like this" or "Mom never did have time to pay attention to anything I had to say. Why would she start now?" If you find yourself getting into such arguments, remind yourself that you are not talking to your real dad or mom now. You are talking to your own inner perceptions of them, and you are in complete control. It is your inner perceptions, not your real parents in the external world, that you need to address. The rest can come later.

While we're on this point, it is interesting to note that time and time again, clients and workshop participants have reported that "miraculous changes" seem to occur in their relationships with their real parents when they come to terms with their own perceptual or "inner parents." This phenomenon seems to prove that most of the time we really don't have to change other people; we only have to change our own minds.

In your own mind, you can create any world you want— and this is the real point of this exercise. By creating your own Self Advocate, you create a perspective of love and mutual respect. It is a perspective that allows you to let go of any blame your Mask Self is telling you to hold on to.

MOVING FORWARD

One of the most important lessons our Self Advocate offers is the realization that it really is possible to become clearer about our own inner guidance, and to trust it more, by working with our own perceptions. As we familiarize ourselves with our Inner Self and our Mask Self, the choices available to us become increasingly clear. We can resolve old conflicts and heal wounds that we are still carrying around inside us. In doing so, we release ourselves from the distortions of the Mask Self that may otherwise victimize us.

It is also important to note that the kind of inner work we're talking about here takes place completely within ourselves, within what we call the Lens of Perception. The Lens of Perception includes our vision of the world, much of which is learned through the experience of day-to-day living.

To follow our bliss, we need to understand how our Lens of Perception affects us, how it influences our decisions, how we can change it, if need be, and how we can focus it so that we are clearer and more trusting about our own inner guidance. In the following chapter, we describe the lens and how it serves us. As you turn to that chapter now, you will recognize many of the themes we've already discussed. It is here, in our discussion of the Lens of Perception, that you'll begin tying together loose ends, providing those final insights for following your bliss.

SEVEN

The Lens of Perception

The human understanding is like a false mirror, which, receiving rays irregularly, distorts and discolors the nature of things by mingling its own nature with it.

—Francis Bacon

How do we change our lives? How do we liberate ourselves from the limitations of the Mask Self so that we can embrace the Inner Self and follow our bliss? We accomplish these things through that part of our minds that we call the "Lens of Perception."

The Lens of Perception is a function of our consciousness that allows us to make sense of the world. Contrary to what most of us would like to think, our senses do not report to us a perfectly accurate or "objective" view of what's really "out there." Rather, our sensory responses go through a filtering process within our minds, during which we consciously or unconsciously assign meanings

136

and give interpretations to data that would otherwise be a meaningless jumble.

The filtering process is carried out by that part of our minds which we here call the Lens of Perception. One of the things we can learn from this is that we can deliberately use this filter to bring about the changes we desire in our lives. In this chapter we'll be discussing exactly how our perceptual abilities work, how this part of our minds not only makes sense of the world, but tends to *project* to the outside world the same world we create inside. It is almost as if we create a script, characters, and situations for a film in our inner world, which we then project to the outer world.

Although there most assuredly is an external world with qualities and characteristics all its own, we tend to discover and attract to us situations in the external world that fill the bill of our inner world. Like motion picture directors putting together a movie, we choose the cast, the script writer, the set designers, the technicians, the musicians, and the actors from an array of virtually unlimited possibilities. The ones we are best able to see and the ones we find most attractive or qualified, those whom we decide to "hire on," are the ones who best fit the plans we've already put together in our minds.

The way the Lens of Perception works is not just a metaphor or a philosophical idea that's fun to play with. Out in the everyday world, the same Lens of Perception causes us to be attracted to the people or the homes or the cars or the jobs we have created in our inner worlds— that is, the world of imagination that exists in our minds. We are attracted to people who appear to fulfill the scripts we have created there as well. Likewise, our inner worlds shape our personalities, give direction to our ways of thinking and acting, our ways of being in the world. And we tend to attract to us people who find that our personalities fulfill scripts they have created in their own minds.

For change to occur in our outer world, we have only

to alter the scripts and characters of our inner worlds. In some ways it is like what happens in a movie theater or on the stage. When you change the finished film in the camera, or you change the script for the characters on the stage, you change the whole atmosphere of that little world you create in the theater. You attract a different crowd, with different likes and dislikes. You interact with them in different ways, and thus, you experience your own life differently.

In this chapter we'll be discussing how the Lens of Perception works in our lives and how we can change it in order to better express the Inner Self so that we can truly follow our bliss.

WHAT'S REALLY OUT THERE?

As we walk across a freshly mowed lawn, we may fully believe that the grass contains the quality of green that we see in our minds, and if we look up, we fully believe that the sky we see really contains the quality of blue. Similarly, the boss we work for really is so difficult that he makes our lives miserable—or on the contrary, our boss is a wonderful person and makes the workaday world a delight.

But what if you were to discover that the world you experience is determined not by what's *out there* but by what's inside you? What if you were to discover that the sky and the grass really contain no color in themselves, but that light reflecting from their surfaces stimulates special sensory organs in your eyes and brain that produce what you experience as a sense of color? And what if you were to discover that regardless of who your boss is, or how he behaves, it is not his behavior, but *your perceptions of his behavior*, that makes your job miserable or a delight?

We depend on the apparent accuracy of our senses and

our perceptions to get us through every day of our lives. We enjoy the fragrant air of a spring day through our sense of smell. We enjoy the feeling of a loved one's hand in ours through our sense of touch. We use our sight to judge safe distances when crossing a street. And we use our perceptual abilities to evaluate new friends, business associates, and the behavior of our children. For the most part, our senses and our perceptions really do work well for us, and because they work so well, it is almost impossible to imagine that the world we see and hear and feel and touch isn't exactly as we perceive it to be. But the fact remains that the grass is not green, and the sky is not blue; rather, our perceptual abilities, from the rods and cones of our eyes to the visual cortex of our brain, paint in the color of these things. Without the miracle of our senses and our perceptions, most of nature would be a drab experience to us.

But what of our perceptions of personal behavior? Certainly there are people and situations that in and of themselves are distasteful or pleasing, exciting or dull, anxiety-producing or calming. And certainly, in the real world, there are people who can make our lives miserable and there are those who can make our lives a delight. But the same principles apply to people as apply to the colors of nature: People behave in ways that are loving or threatening, but our own perceptions of them are what's responsible for creating our experience of misery or pleasure.

Does this mean that we have complete control over every situation we find ourselves in? Does it mean that we can change other people's behavior by changing our perceptions of them? No, it simply isn't that easy. However, it does mean that we can take responsibility for our perceptions, and as we do this, we can cease being victims and start taking care of ourselves lovingly and constructively, even in the most unpleasant circumstances. We can begin to appreciate ourselves more, since we now realize

how marvelous we humans really are. Our Creator has
endowed us with the gift of perception, which allows us
to enjoy our world and take an active role in its ongoing
creation.

YOUR LENS, MY LENS

Each one of us sees the world in a slightly different
way. It is as though we each hold up a lens through which
we must look in order to get the world into focus, or in
order to make sense of the myriad sensations that the
world stimulates in us. This lens is by no means bright
and clear. Instead, it is filled with images and impressions,
blind spots and colorations, that are the sum total of our
life experiences. At any moment, as we gaze out at the
world through this lens, it is difficult to tell what is in the
lens, and what is a part of the external world itself.

We (Susan and Hal) may be looking at the same sunset
but be seeing entirely different things. Let's say, for example, that the two of us happen to be together at the
ocean on the anniversary of the day when Susan's parents'
house burned down, many years before. She is recalling
this event with great sadness, and as the sun sets, she
cannot help but be reminded of it. She may only notice
the tumultuous reds and yellows as the sun disappears
behind the horizon, matching in her own mind the sad and
terrifying image of her family home burning to the ground
when she was a child. Awhile before this, as she went out
to watch the sunset, she may have just received the news
that a very dear friend of hers is moving to another city,
and she is already mourning the loss of closeness she had
shared with this person. All these concerns become images
in the lens through which she views the sunset, and without her even thinking about it, they will be projected to
what she sees there.

Sitting beside her, Hal may notice only the soft hues of

orange that blend into the darkening sky, and for him the
sunset brings up pleasant memories of his childhood, of
spending warm evenings with family and friends around
the fireplace at his parents' home. At the same time, he
has just received the news that a book he has written has
gotten a rave review in a prestigious magazine, and that
wonderful news brightens the lens through which he views
the sunset.

In our minds, the experiences of the sunset that evening
will always be different, though we were sitting in the
same place and gazing out over the same horizon at exactly the same time of day.

Alfred North Whitehead, the American mathematician
and scholar, noted this same phenomenon when he said:
"The mind in apprehending also experiences sensations
which, properly speaking, are qualities of the mind alone.
These sensations are projected by the mind so as to clothe
appropriate bodies in external nature. Thus the bodies are
perceived as with qualities which in reality do not belong
to them, qualities which in fact are purely the offspring
of the mind. Thus nature gets the credit which should in
truth be reserved for ourselves: the rose for its scent; the
nightingale for its song; and the sun for its radiance."

In a very real sense, we might say that the lens of perception *distorts* the reality of the external world, or *im-
poses a personal meaning* onto it that the external world
does not, in itself, possess. At first glance, we may protest
such distortions, insisting that we must learn to accurately
interpret the truth about what is really out there. However, as we shall soon see, evidence points to the fact that
we are bound to our distortions and projections. Further-
more, without this ability to project our realities, we cannot make sense of our life experience. Without these
abilities, the myriad sensations pouring into our consciousnesses every moment of the day would probably drive us
to distraction, and we would lose our ability to think and
act.

In medical history, there are cases of people who, through physical trauma, have lost the cognitive function that helps them interpret sensations. These people spend their days totally occupied with the sights and sounds, smells, tastes, and tactile sensations that speed through their nervous systems endlessly. They are unable to speak, act, or take care of themselves because they have no way of organizing all the sensory data that bombards their minds.

Down through history, there have been a great many efforts to come to terms with this lens, to free ourselves of its influence so that we might better understand what is *really* out there. In some Eastern religions, there has been a traditional effort to clear the lens, to remove its distortions through mental disciplines such as meditation. To some extent, it is possible to achieve a state of relative objectivity through these techniques. But there is a certain irony in all this, too. As the French writer Alain pointed out, "A mind that could know the object-world without error would know nothing at all."

Western science has made similar efforts to peek around the lens, to stop the projections and attempt to objectivize what is really there. Where the Eastern disciplines use meditation to achieve this objectivity, scientists use mental tools such as double-blind studies, reason, math, the microscope, and statistics. With the advancement of particle physics, however, scientists began to see that their own presence, the mass of particles that they identified as their own physical bodies, had to be included as part of that lens, and thus part of the distortion. They found that in spite of employing the best tools for achieving objectivity, the observer's own presence changed the nature of the thing being observed. This led the German physicist Ludwig Boltzmann to comment in *Theoretical Physics and Philosophical Problems* that:

"My observation has not only recorded reality. I am much more than an objective observer, since my presence, the presence of the particles that make up my very being, alters that reality."

There is a third approach to the lens, one that is shared by the shamanic traditions and some of the Eastern religions. The point of view we find here is that we can come to terms with the distortions only by looking directly into the lens itself. We gain relative freedom from our distortions by getting to know what is in the lens and learning to distinguish what is there from what is in the world outside the lens.

An example from real life helps to illustrate how this works:

Throughout my (Hal's) life, any form of rejection, from a turndown of a manuscript to the anger of anyone with whom I felt a close bond, nearly always resulted in my feeling abandoned. At such times I felt extremely alone and without support, as if there were no one to whom I could turn for comfort or help with my feelings. In extreme cases, this was accompanied by tension in my stomach and shoulders and a profound light-headedness that sometimes made it difficult to think. Many times when this occurred, I was unable to describe what I was feeling or if I was feeling anything at all. It seemed to me that I had been anesthetized and separated from my feelings. I frequently felt helpless in the face of it, and often the only thing I believed I could do was to hide out and nurse my wounds until these feelings passed.

Usually these episodes would last for a few minutes or for as long as an hour, although occasionally they lasted for a day or two. During that period of time, I perceived my discomfort as having been *caused* by the rejection of my writing efforts or by the person who expressed anger toward me. In other words, I often projected my feelings of abandonment to the event of rejection or anger, and saw it as responsible for my turmoil. In this way, I literally created a world in which I was left alone and without support from other people whenever I encountered rejection or anger. Then one day, in a conversation with my mother, I discovered the following about myself, which gave me a new way of seeing the world.

My mother told me that when I was born, there were medical complications and she was given a general anesthetic. Because she was anesthetized, the doctors assisted my birth with forceps, and at the time I was actually born, my mother was unconscious. I was then sent to the nursery, which was a common practice in those days.

The following morning, with both of us still groggy from the anesthetic, I was brought to my mother to be fed. However, she rejected me, because during the time *she* was out, she dreamed that my father had come to her and told her that she had given birth to a girl. As a result of her conviction that I was someone else's baby, I lay in the nursery for the entire first day of my life, and on into the next, until my father returned from a short business trip and convinced Mother that the baby the hospital had given her was really hers.

As I was told this story for the first time, I became aware that I was vividly reliving all the feelings of abandonment that I must have felt as an infant. I was surprised to recognize how similar they were to the feelings I experienced whenever I received a turndown from a publisher or was confronted with the anger of a loved one. And at that moment I realized that these feelings were not *caused* by events in the external world. They were part of the life experience contained in my lens, superimposed on any event that seemed similar in content to that earliest experience of rejection and abandonment. It was almost as though the early experience worked like the film in a movie projector, casting old images of abandonment over any event that even remotely resembled those old feelings.

When the past was projected into the present in this way, it did much more than simply distort the external event: It also created a world in my mind that was based on that earliest experience of abandonment. It was a world in which I felt helpless and dependent (the memory of being an infant), a world in which there was no warmth or comfort, a world where in spite of my own naive efforts to call attention to my plight, no one responded or seemed to have the capacity to satisfy my needs or help reduce the discomfort I was experiencing.

As these old memories rolled through my mind, their images and themes were also projected to the world outside me. The world I saw *out there* was a world very much like the one I saw in my own mind. For example, I was quite capable of transforming other people's expressions of confusion about how to help me into a very convincing picture, in my mind, that they wanted nothing to do with me. I—not the other person—was responsible for creating the rejection and abandonment I felt.

But then a very interesting thing happened. I was able to see that I was like the operator in the projection booth of a movie theater, and I had a choice about which film I loaded into my projector or put into my lens. Thereafter, I was able to remind myself that my perceptions of the world were just that—perceptions, old films, distortions of the external reality created out of my own life experiences. It became possible, when I saw this, to begin taking responsibility for my interpretation, or distortion, of the events that occurred in my life. I began to see, for example, that the pain of abandonment was not caused by the external world: Rather, it was caused by my own perceptions and my body's memory of that first painful encounter with abandonment.

Once we are able to accept responsibility for creating our own worlds in this way, we can begin creating perceptions that work better for us. I (Hal), for example, began seeking ways to create an inner world that was more supportive, a world in which I could ask for help in getting through periods when I felt abandoned and separated from my own feelings. By creating the supportive inner world, I began to find that same support in the external world. And every time I experienced this more satisfying and supportive world, it added a new element to my lens of perception, new scenes and new characters for the movie I projected out onto the world.

Every one of us does a similar thing every time we open our minds to new experiences. At those moments of great peace, when we are pleased with ourselves and feeling secure, we are most likely to take in information or recognize a different kind of relationship with the people around us. When this happens, we automatically expand the perceptual world within our own minds, and in turn, we begin creating new possibilities in our interactions with the external world.

CREATED IN OUR OWN IMAGE AND LIKENESS

Much of the time, of course, we do not have time to sit back and consider these more complex views of reality. Instead, we think and act as if that which we perceive is the only truth there is. In this state, which can be described as "innocence," we are unable to see that the Lens of Perception is even there, or that experiences from our pasts shade how we view the present. In its most comic proportions, this is the Quixotic life, one of "tilting at windmills" with the legendary Don Quixote, fighting battles with enemies that don't exist, falling in love with phantom lovers, and these experiences generally end up being confusing, disappointing, and occasionally tragic. It is a way of looking at the world that guarantees that we will feel everything is out of control, since the world *out there* is always imposing a different reality than the one we perceive.

EXAMPLES FROM THE PAST

There is a wonderful story which Geoffrey Chaucer, the author of *The Canterbury Tales*, tells in his poem "The Parliament of Fowls." The story in the poem takes place in the kingdom of birds. We are told that the falcon is coming of age, and his father has called together all the birds of the kingdom to advise him in choosing a mate.

Each bird, in turn, is given a chance to speak. The duck advises that the falcon should choose a mate with webbed feet, since this virtue will allow her to paddle through the water at great speed and to walk in the mud at the edge of ponds, where she may seek out the tasty morsels to be found there. The swan advises the falcon that he should choose a mate with a long, graceful neck, not only because it is beautiful, but because it allows one to dip deep into the water and select out minnows or tadpoles for its supper. The nightingale similarly extols the virtues of marrying a bird who can sing a melodious song. And so it goes, with each bird extolling the virtues of its own kind and advising the falcon accordingly.

In the end the falcon thanks each bird, and tells them that together they have taught him an important lesson. He has noticed how each one of them has seen the ideal mate as being one that matches his or her own image. And he sees that this is the lesson, that each must choose according to his own image of what is truest and strongest and most beautiful in himself.

In this is a lesson for us when we are looking at our own Lens of Perception. The lens casts only a partial truth upon the external world. The images, shadows, and colors it projects tell us more about ourselves than they tell about the external world. If there is a common truth to be seen in all this, it is only that each one of us projects his or her own world, and that what we see in our Lens of Perception is our own creation. Our explanations of events outside us can accurately be seen only as mirrors of who we are, reflecting the events that have shaped our lives.

In Robert Browning's poem "The Imprisoned Splendour," he says: "Truth is within ourselves, it takes no rise/ From outward things, whate'er you may believe..."

THE WORLD AS MALLEABLE

Each person's life experience is shaped inside his or her own lens. The house and neighborhood where I grew up are different from the ones where you grew up, and those differences go into shaping the world we experience—both in the past and now. The faces I see in my mind, and the relationships I experience when I hear the words "mom" and "dad," are quite different from the ones you may see, and those differences, too, shape how we experience the world.

No two people can possibly share exactly the same lens, not even when they are identical twins who have hardly left each other's sides. Brought up in different locales, being physically different, being constitutionally sensitive to different things—so also will our lenses contain different imagery by which we make sense of the world. Even if we were able to duplicate every experience two people have had, it would not be possible to duplicate how they put all the ingredients together in their separate minds.

When working with the inner world of the Lens of Perception, it is important to recognize that the imagery is quite plastic—that it is quite malleable and can be changed. It can be assembled in any number of ways. Whole scenes can be edited and put together so that they make a different kind of sense than they originally did. This allows you to project a different perception of the external world and to finally experience your life in a different way, hopefully one more of your own choosing.

We know that in using techniques such as the "power of positive thinking," we can learn to project an image of optimism and faith that you will get what you desire and turn ordinarily negative experiences into positive and nurturing ones.

People tend to want to cooperate with others who act and think in a positive way. Positive thinking is simple enough: Before making a call, for example, a salesman creates an image in his or her mind of the customer greeting him openly and asking him to write out a large order. Or the college student, nervous about asking out a young man she has just met, creates an image in her mind of the object of her attention being flattered and accepting her invitation cheerfully. In a great many cases, the results created in the lens do come true in the real world: The salesman writes up a big order, and the college student's young man accepts her invitation.

The power of positive thinking works well for relatively simple communications. But we can go beyond that. Through the Lens of Perception, we see things that are not, strictly speaking, a part of the external world. These may be fears evoked by something that has occurred in the external world, but belonging only to the observer. They might be hopes prompted by opportunities seen in external events.

Hopes and fears may appear in the lens in many different forms, and as they do, they may begin to influence our own actions and the actions of others: The jealous lover, fearing his mate's infidelity, may create mental images of his mate in the arms of another man; or the entrepreneur, hopeful of great success in her new venture, may create mental images of her business expanding into a multimillion-dollar corporation.

The mental images created in our Lens of Perception guide and direct our actions and our ways of relating to the world. The entrepreneur's images of success motivate her to seek out people and resources to literally make her dream come true. Her enthusiasm and faith are infectious, and they encourage others to support her. On the negative side, the jealous lover consciously or unconsciously seeks signs of his mate's infidelity, and the mate becomes resentful of the apparent distrust in the relationship. Resentments build, creating a wall between them, and the jealous mate's worst fears eventually do come true.

Reflecting on the malleable nature of reality, and how it can be shaped by the world we create within our Lens of Perception, Abraham Maslow noted that:

> A husband's conviction that his wife is beautiful, or a wife's firm belief that her husband is courageous, to some extent *creates* the beauty or the courage. This is not so much a perception of something that already exists as a bringing into existence by belief. Shall we perhaps consider this an example of perception of potentiality, since *every* person has the possibility of being beautiful or courageous?

So in addition to shaping the reality we perceive, the world in the lens influences the world outside us, bringing about change that matches or approximates the inner world. Where the lover's perception of his mate is a positive one, it may encourage growth and the development of those qualities in the other. Where a manager has a perception that there is good in everyone, he tends to find it and encourage his employees to bring out that good. These positive perceptions can have the effect of actualizing potentialities in people and situations outside ourselves, much like turning on a light in a dark room.

The opposite is also true, of course. A person's self-growth can be limited by nonsupportive relationships. From child development studies, we know that the child whose parents are forever focusing on his or her faults tends to develop those faults, and the child whose parents are forever focusing on his or her strengths and innate talents tends to develop those strengths and talents.

THE MASK SELF WITHIN THE LENS

The Mask Self is, for the most part, a self-image, contained in the lens, that has been created from our own perceptions of other people's (mostly our parents') perceptions of us. As such, the Mask Self is not *carved in granite*—that is, it is a perception, an image in our inner world. As adults, we can identify our own Mask Self and ultimately make subtle changes that allow us to experience the world in very different ways.

The Mask Self need not dominate the actions, perceptions, and experiences of our lives. We can, for example, bring up the spotlight on the Inner Self and allow it to become a stronger part of the picture we project to the external world. The process is not one of pretending something that may or may not be so, as the salesman might do when he creates an image of success in his mind on a day when he is really feeling pessimistic and low. Rather, it is a process of learning how to carry on a conversation with the Inner Self, or in some other way giving it greater recognition. As it emerges, the Inner Self can change the entire picture on your Lens of Perception.

In light of these realizations about the Lens of Perception, a very different view of our lives begins to emerge. First and foremost, it becomes easier to begin operating from the belief that personal power has its roots in our minds.

If we are feeling powerless in our present lives, it is because we, through our lens and its projections, are creating that powerlessness and projecting it outside us. This is not to say that we have deliberately chosen these projections. However, once we begin to see the specific ways in which we are creating that world of powerlessness, and some of the benefits we once may have derived from this powerlessness, we find that we do have choices, and we can change the way we feel and act in the world. We can learn to create other images to project, images that will offer deep satisfaction and the fulfillment of our fondest dreams.

As though reflecting directly on these possibilities, the poet Wallace Stevens in his poem, "The Necessary Angel," said, "Reality is not that external scene but the life that is lived in it." Stevens, perhaps more than any other American poet, had great insights into the nature of human perception, and he made it the subject of most of his work. In light of this, it is interesting to note that he wrote most of his poems, some of which are now classics in American literature, in the backseat of the private limousine that drove him to and from the office, where he carried out his duties as president of one of our country's largest insurance companies!

LIVING WITH OUR OWN CREATIONS

When we think about the effects of our inner worlds on our lives in the external world, it may be a little frightening to contemplate. If we are to accept the possibility that we base our ideas and actions on models we possess within our Lens of Perception, then we also have to accept that it is impossible to blame the external world for what we consider our failures, our lack of luck, our most difficult relationships, and even, perhaps, our health problems. All of these may well have their most important causes within us.

But a word of caution is due here. We believe that the concept that "we each create our own world" through our inner perceptions is an oversimplification of the way the world works. Remember that just as I am creating my own world, so are you and several other millions of people creating theirs. There is often a point where some or all of these creations merge in a kind of synergy of perceptions, producing a much larger collective perception that affects each and every one of us in ways that no single person could ever quite predict.

We find an excellent example of this synergy in large issues such as the environmental crisis. Whereas you might create an inner world model of a clean and healthy environment, you are not alone. Others have inner world models for making chemicals and other products that also have an impact on the environment. And remember, all the problems we face today began generations ago, with ideas that, at the time, may have seemed not only benign but beneficial. The bottom line is that no single one of us can bring about changes on our own; no single person has complete control.

If there is a fallacy in the notion that we each create our own worlds, it is also a very constructive and necessary fallacy. To follow our bliss, we must take a leap of faith. We must recognize that even though we don't have total control of the external world, or any person in it, we do have a great deal of control where our own inner worlds are concerned. When we recognize how much our inner worlds really do affect the quality of our lives in the external world, it seems like pure folly not to take as much responsibility as we can for creating the most delightful, joyous, harmonious, and loving inner worlds possible. Ultimately the external world does mirror our inner worlds.

According to many psychologists, most of the concepts and the imagery of our individualized inner worlds were created before we were five years of age. This means that we form many of our perceptions long before we have enough information to make reasonable judgments about our experiences. The child of an alcoholic parent, for example, doesn't know that all parents aren't emotionally or physically abusive to their children. Certainly as infants, the children of alcoholic parents lack the perspective to say to themselves, "I should not have to be subjected to the dangers of riding around in this car with a drunk mother" or "I have done nothing to deserve the emotional abuse my father is heaping on us all right now."

Because the knowledge we need for understanding our experiences is so limited in our formative years, the perceptions we develop are usually little more than misunderstandings. We each grow up with a Lens of Perception filled with half-truths, and what one workshop participant described as "foggy reckonings," at best.

All too many of us limit ourselves to these early perceptions. We go through our lives barely questioning the impressions we have of the world. For example, the anxiety about money which we may have learned from a parent in our early years becomes, in our own unquestioned minds, a basic truth about the world. Then, in adulthood, we put all our energy into acquiring more and more money, firmly convinced that we can literally buy our freedom from that anxiety in this way. The trouble is that for such a person, peace of mind can't be purchased. It can only be gotten by identifying and healing the source of the original anxiety.

Similarly, the fear of close relationships which we learned from our parents when we were small children may become a basic truth for us in adulthood, and we find ourselves getting into one relationship after another with people who are not trustworthy. The impression we get from our adult experiences may lead us to say, "You see, this is proof that my perceptions are right! People really aren't trustworthy." The underlying truth eludes us—that our own perceptions have literally magnetized us to the destructive relationships we most fear. Our external reality is merely mirroring our inner one.

Lucky for all of us that our perceptions aren't static! We aren't just stuck with whatever perceptions we absorbed in our youth. As long as we have the willingness to do so, we can create new perceptions and change old ones. The power to do this begins with observing how our inner worlds shape our outer worlds.

EXPERIENTIAL EXERCISE:
OBSERVING HOW YOUR INNER WORLD
SHAPES THE OUTER WORLD

Purpose: The purpose of this exercise is to allow you to see how your Lens of Perception affects the physical world. You will see from this that your presence in the world, and the existence of your inner world, really does make a difference, a difference that we often don't see for ourselves.

This exercise is done while sitting at home, in a place where you feel at ease, comfortable with yourself and your surroundings. The room should be one that contains objects that you have chosen and brought into your life.

Instructions: Look around you and take the time to carefully study everything you see. Let your eyes wander over the surface of things, as though seeing them for the first time. Especially focus your attention on anything that you were directly responsible for choosing or bringing to this place. If there are things that you have made yourself, acknowledge these to yourself. If you arranged the furniture in this room, if you hung pictures on the walls, or if you were responsible for any of these getting done, note that to yourself.

Close your eyes and pretend that all these things, and the room in which you are sitting, exists only in your Lens of Perception. Let yourself enjoy it all only as an image in your inner world.

Acknowledge your part in the creation of this image with a thought such as "I have created all this. I have brought all this into my life, and I have created the pleasure I enjoy in them."

At first, this self-affirmation may seem unbelievable or absurd. After all, you have probably not made the couch or the chair you're sitting on. You have probably not put up the walls that form the perimeter of this room. How then could you have created all this?

Think about our discussion in this chapter, and recognize that even though you (probably) have not created the room and every object in it, you have created the inner image of it, the world you are now seeing in your Lens of Perception.

Note also that the objects you enjoy in this room would not have been present in this place, or in this particular order, had it not been for your involvement with them. It does not matter how the objects came to you, whether as gifts from friends or your own purchases. This space, where you now sit, would not have been possible without your perceptions, without your participation in their creation.

You are the difference!

Now think about something you have created or accomplished, either on your own or with the help of other people. This could be something at work. It could be the organization of a vacation trip that went particularly well. It could be your contribution as a parent, or your participation in working out conflicts with a mate or coworker.

Recall the earliest part of this accomplishment, remembering when it was only an idea or a hope or a dream inside your own Lens of Perception. Focus on this moment, and then realize that the final accomplishment began as this seed or feeling that you created in your inner world. Without this seed and the actions you took, that accomplishment could never have become a reality.

You make the difference!

Think about a relationship you have had with one other person in your life. Let yourself recall a time when the two of you shared a moment of great pleasure. Recall what you were thinking or feeling at that moment. Recognize that the world you created in your Lens of Perception made this moment possible, and your friend's pleasure would not have been the same without your participation.

You make the difference!

This exercise is a subtle one. You may not immediately feel any dramatic results from doing it. But each time you repeat it, your appreciation of the power you possess through your Lens of Perception will increase. Take the time, while going through a normal day of activities, to look at your world the way you did in this exercise. As you do this, you will have a natural tendency to value your own contribution in the world more, and to see the world you create in your Lens of Perception as a major resource in every situation where you are involved.

MOVING FORWARD

Up to now, we've been looking at the basic mechanisms of human consciousness that affect us as we pursue life paths that are inner-directed. In the pages ahead, we turn to the practical portion of this book, that is, the workbook section, where we begin applying these concepts in our own lives. The goal of the entire workbook section is to offer a step-by-step plan for clarifying and "turning up the volume" of that voice within each one of us that tells us how to follow our bliss.

THE
Workbook Section

Workbook Contents

OVERVIEW

The Workbook

In this part of the book, we present a step-by-step program to help you construct a road map for following your bliss, using the principles we've described.

The program consists of seven preliminary steps, with an eighth step that puts it all together. This eighth step allows you to put your work to the test by applying this new knowledge to a real-world problem or challenge with which you are presently confronted. For those who wish to go further than this, there are two brief exercises for putting together plans to follow your bliss in your personal relations and in your life work.

In addition to being steps in a program, the mental tools we present here can be used independently. They can be applied as decision-making tools and for everyday problem solving.

Each step is organized as follows:

1. The Number and Name of the Step
This consists of the number of the step and a self-explanatory title.

2. The Purpose of the Step

A brief statement about what you will gain by taking this step.

3. Background of the Benefits

A discussion of the overall benefits of this step, both in the short and long terms, and any background material that will help clarify how the step works.

4. The Instructions

Simply that—the instructions for carrying out this step.

5. An Example

In cases where it seemed to us it would be helpful to the reader, we provide an example.

6. An Assignment

To fully *ground* the knowledge you gain from these steps, it is important to begin applying it in real-life situations. The assignments we describe suggest ways for you to do this.

In the early chapters of this book, we suggested that you keep a journal and record any work you did and any ideas you had as you went along. From time to time we noted that we would be asking you to refer to journal notes you made. You'll find that in the steps described in this workbook, there are instructions for how you'll be able to use those previously recorded notes. But don't worry if you didn't complete that earlier work, or if you lost it. We also provide instructions for catching up.

STEP ONE

The Homing Device

THE PURPOSE OF THIS STEP

In this first step you will be creating a mental tool for reading and interpreting the subtlest messages from your Inner Self. This "Homing Device," which we first described very briefly in Chapter 1, will provide you with a dependable scale for making decisions and choices that help you follow your bliss.

BACKGROUND OF THE BENEFITS

For just a moment, imagine how it would be to have this Homing Device within you. This device has a single dedicated purpose: to tell you when you are on a path that will lead you to the fulfillment of your life purpose, and when you are straying from that path. In short, its single purpose is to tell you when you are following your bliss.

Imagine how easy it would be to make choices and decisions if you had such a device within you. All you'd have to do is take a few seconds to consult it whenever you were faced with a problem or had a decision to make in your life. In considering a new job, it would instantly tell you whether that job was on your path or off it. It would indicate to you whether that job was only a temporary means to an end or a position that would take you closer to finding your life purpose. In working out problems in your relationships, you could check out solutions and see if they would release you from your feelings of conflict, or deepen them.

The purpose of this part of our program is to explore ways to read the subtlest signals from our homing devices, long before they have become physical symptoms, major emotional conflicts, or health problems. We suggest that it is possible to learn how to read the signals when they are still gentle whispers and while the course for getting back on the path to follow our bliss can still be corrected with a simple thought or a word.

THE INSTRUCTIONS

Begin by visualizing the following "Readout" scale in your mind:

$$[-10 \ -8 \ -6 \ -4 \ -2 \ <0> \ +2 \ +4 \ +6 \ +8 \ +10]$$

Here's how it works.

The right side of the scale represents positive messages, that is, all the feelings that you associate with experiences that are on the blissful side of life. For example, a Positive 10 would include everything you experience during a peak experience, as we discussed in Chapter 2. Conversely, a Negative 10 would include everything you associate with an Essential Wound, as we discussed in Chapters 5 and 6.

Each person should "program" the Readout scale individually. To program the positive side of the scale, let yourself go back in time to a peak experience from your past. Get in touch with what you were thinking and feeling at that time, and make a list to which you can refer at a later date, should you wish to do so.

Here's how this might look:

Positive Readout List

1. I felt totally in touch with my body.
2. I felt relaxed, but I was also alert and fully aware of everything going on around me.
3. Although I wasn't thinking very deeply about anything in particular, my attention was completely focused on what I was doing.
4. I had the sense that there was no separation between me and what I was doing.
5. I felt completely certain about what I was doing, that at this moment I was on the path, doing exactly what I should be doing with my life.

List as many items as you wish, with as much detail as you wish. After completing this list, go on and do one for the negative side of the scale. This time, of course, you'll be focusing on negative experiences from your past, such as an Essential Wound or other key negative experiences you have had. That list might look something like this:

Negative Readout List

1. I feel frustrated and angry.
2. All the muscles in my back and neck are knotted up, and I really feel like hitting someone.
3. My heart is pounding and I am hyperventilating.
4. I have this overriding sense that "I just don't want to be here now." I want to run as fast as I can in the other direction.
5. I want to cry out for help, but I am afraid if I do, I will only expose myself to getting hurt even more.

When you are done programming the positive and negative scales, get in touch with how it feels to be at the zero point between these scales. In other words, how would it be to feel neither positive or negative, but simply at ease and at rest? You may have experienced this while just beginning to relax or meditate. Or perhaps you experienced it immediately after completing a routine task at home or on the job.

You now have your Readout scale completely "programmed." The next step is to test it with a real-life situation. To do this, bring to your mind a recent decision you've made or an action you've taken that involves your job or a relationship. Allow yourself to recall how you felt then, what you were thinking, and any other parts of the experience that come to mind. Recall as many details as you can: the tone of people's voices, the color of the rug on the floor, whether you felt warm or hot, and so forth. Then rate your experience, either positive or negative, on the Readout scale.

For now, just note your ratings. We'll be doing more with these ratings in the following steps.

AN EXAMPLE

Two days before coming to the workshop, Rick had a conflict with a coworker whom we'll call Betty. He became angry with her because he had to complete a time-consuming job that had been her responsibility. It was not the first time this had come up, so Rick, as he described it, "had really been steamed."

When he confronted Betty with the problem, she had a ready excuse. She told him she had been overloaded with work that day and there were several jobs, not just the one in question, that she had to put off. She apologized and told Rick that it would never happen again. At that time, Rick accepted the apology, but a few minutes later he was feeling resentful, certain that he had been manipulated.

We asked Rick to stop for a moment, take a deep breath, exhale slowly, and relax. Then we asked him to imagine his Readout scale and check to see how he was feeling about that decision to accept Betty's apology.

He closed his eyes, relaxed, and imagined the scale. A second later he said, "I'd have to place it about three or four on the negative side. The situation upsets me, but I'm not so angry that I am ready to do anything more about it."

We then asked him, "Would you say that the choice you made to accept Betty's apology was following your bliss?"

Rick applied the Readout scale to this question. Instantly he shook his head. "No doubt about that. It's about a six on the negative side. It absolutely wasn't okay."

"Can you imagine a situation with Betty where you might feel that the way you handled the problem could be perfectly on track for you, a definite positive on the scale, and that you are following your bliss?"

He stopped and thought for a moment. "Yes. I think what would be on target for me would be if I had started back a couple days, when it first happened. I waited too long. When I first saw that she wasn't doing her job, I should have gone to her and told her right then and there. I should have made certain she took care of things right when they happened. I shouldn't have done her work for her."

"And if you'd done that, you would have felt that you were following your bliss?"

Rick nodded. He added that one of the problems he had in his life was that he was always trying to please other people. He often ended up feeling that others took advantage of him. He was in a management training program and knew that he had to learn how to set limits on how much he extended himself to others. Recently he had found that when he made demands on others and established truly cooperative working relationships, he felt great about himself and his coworkers. But it was still difficult for him to do what he had to do to bring this about.

Rick's story is instructive to all of us for two reasons: First, his use of the Readout scale helped him to become more aware of how his way of handling the situation with Betty was affecting him on a deeper level. It was not simply an annoyance to him. The deeper truth for Rick was that the choice he made to accept her apology took him off the path of moving toward creating more cooperative working relationships. Second, his use of the Homing Device allowed him to stand back and take a look at how he might have handled the situation so that he would feel that he was staying on his path and following his bliss.

AN ASSIGNMENT

Begin using your Homing Device to check out some of the choices and decisions you are making in your life right now. At work or at home, be aware of the fact that every time you feel a challenge or a problem arising, this is an opportunity to do a Readout and check out actions or decisions before you make them.

Simply stop for a moment, take a deep breath or two, exhaling slowly as you relax. Then picture the Readout scale of your Homing Device and rate your feelings. If you rate yourself on the negative side of the scale, or very low on the positive side, ask yourself what you might do to feel better. Is there a way of handling the situation you're facing so that you will come out feeling on the high, positive, *blissful* side of the scale? For now, simply do this in your mind.

Whenever you see the opportunity for it, do a Readout of your activities with your Homing Device. Get into the habit of using the Homing Device for everything from minor decisions, such as what to buy for dinner, to major ones, such as resolving relationship and career problems.

This is only the first phase of using your Homing Device to follow your bliss. There's more to come.

STEP TWO

Readouts of the Mask Self

THE PURPOSE OF THIS STEP

You'll be exploring how to use your Homing Device to alert you to times when you are seeing the world through the eyes of your Mask Self, which can blind you to the true path for following your bliss.

BACKGROUND OF THE BENEFITS

In Chapter 5, we discussed how the Mask Self nearly always leads us off our true paths. Our first reaction when we discover this comes directly from the Mask Self. In its own defense, it will send us messages such as, "Don't pay any attention to this stuff. You've got to listen to me and do what I tell you. Sometimes you just can't follow your bliss, and this is one of those times."

The greater your resistance, and the stronger you hear these kinds of arguments from your Mask Self, the more you can be sure that you are on the right track. The more you can be sure that you are being limited by choices made not by your Inner Self but by your Mask Self. Let the negative readings signal you to take a closer look at your Mask Self and see how it is mirrored in your present conflict.

THE INSTRUCTIONS

Choose a situation in your life where you have consistently felt conflict, lack of harmony, or anger. This might involve a relationship problem or a problem you are having in your work. It is best to choose a situation where you have felt that you really had no alternative but to do what you did. Perhaps you felt that the position you took was extremely important to you. You may have felt that your personal integrity or honor were at stake. Or you felt that the lack of understanding on the other person's part deeply hurt you.

For a moment, put yourself back into the conflict. Check out your own feelings using the Readout scale from Step One. If you get a high negative reading on the scale, say, in the range between 5 and 10, recognize that your Homing Device is trying to tell you that your Mask Self, rather than your Inner Self, is affecting your decisions and choices where this situation is concerned. And remember, your Mask Self always leads you off your true path, further and further from following your bliss!

Make any notes you wish to make about how your Mask Self is influencing your choices in the situation you've just explored with your Homing Device. Look at similarities between the present situation where you feel in conflict or challenged, and any experiences in your past when you felt hurt, confused, or personally discounted.

It is important to remind yourself of what happens when there appear to be strong similarities between the present situations and your experiences from the past; your Mask Self will distort the present. When this happens, the other person is unable to understand what is upsetting you. After all, the cause of your upset at this moment is as much attached to the past as to the present.

Remind yourself that when we are looking through the eyes of the Mask Self, we are seeing the world through many filters. We are seeing not just the present, but many layers of the old wounds. It is just like projecting images of the past onto the present through a slide or movie projector. It becomes very difficult to sort out the difference between the projected images from the past and the images of the present reality. Old material from the Essential Wound colors the present with pain, confusion, anger, feelings of abandonment, loss of self-worth, and other unpleasant feelings that really belong only to the past.

AN EXAMPLE

The following story about Kris and James illustrates how this process can work in real life. It tells how you might take the step past conflict to gain new freedom from the Mask Self, and greater trust in the guidance of your Inner Self.

In the beginning of their relationship, Kris thoroughly enjoyed taking care of James, fixing up their apartment, doing the shopping, the cooking, and the cleaning. And of course, James thoroughly enjoyed having Kris take care of him in this way.

As the months passed, however, tensions mounted. They both had jobs away from home, though Kris worked only part-time, while James worked full-time at a regular job. Kris began complaining that James never did anything around the house, that he acted as if he were superior to her and felt that he shouldn't have to do such menial work.

James was deeply hurt by Kris's complaints. He said

that in the beginning she had seemed to get as much pleasure out of doing the housework as he got out of having
her care for him in these ways. Besides, he argued, since
he was working full-time, and she only half-time, her
doing the housework had seemed like a fair division of
labor.

Without trying to resolve whether or not the young couple had a fair division of labor, we asked Kris to recall the
last time she felt resentful toward James for all the housework she had to do. This was easy for her, since the last
time this happened was the same morning the couple
came in to see us.

We then asked Kris to rate how she felt on the Readout
scale. When she did this, she came out with a Negative
8, a very high negative reading. She began talking about
this, saying that although she knew she was bothered by
this problem, she had not realized that she was bothered
that much.

The question we always ask ourselves when we find that
we are doing something that is not following our bliss is
"Why? What is it within ourselves that reinforces our belief that we must follow such a path?"

Kris's first response to this question was that she felt it
was her duty, that since James was providing the main
support for the two of them, she should be doing her part
in the marriage by keeping house. Kris saw that there
were alternatives. James and she had discussed her working a few extra hours each week so that they could hire a
housekeeper to do the heavier work. But she didn't feel
right about doing this, either.

In Kris's case, that insight came to her very quickly.
Raised in a family with three older brothers, she had felt
completely intimidated, just as her mother had. Her father
had spent a great deal of time with the boys, taking them
hunting and fishing, taking them to sports events, and
encouraging them all to excel in activities that were generally considered "macho." Kris described herself as a

"second-class citizen" in the family, because she was not a boy. Her brothers teased her unmercifully, and her father barely acknowledged her existence. The one time she felt safe was when she was helping her mother with housework. It was then that she got some personal recognition and a sense that she was a valued member of the family. Her mother deeply appreciated her help, and the time they spent doing this work together was really quality time for Kris. She felt close to her mother, even though they both resented the way the rest of the family looked upon them as second-class citizens, or as little more than servants.

Kris described her mask as "Mother's Little Helper," and even as she spoke these words aloud, she became resentful. Her stomach knotted up and she felt angry. She felt that she was not being seen for who she really was. Nor was she seeing the broad possibilities of her relationship with James, which went far beyond the limited relationship that seemed to be presented to her through the eyes of her Mask Self.

AN ASSIGNMENT

During the next few days, use your Homing Device to do readouts of any of your regular activities. This can be anything from wearing certain clothes to going to your particular job each day. If you find any areas of your life where you get consistently high negative readings—meaning negative readings between 5 and 10—recognize that this indicates high involvement with your Mask Self. These are areas where you are clearly not following your bliss.

If you need to do so, go back and read Chapter 5, "Masks That Hide the Inner Self," to remind you of how this aspect of your life works. Then, just as Kris and other people in our examples have done, give your Mask Self a name: Kris called her Mask Self "Mother's Little Helper." Back in Chapter 5, we called Joel's Mask Self "The Quiet Nice Guy." Invent a name, or pick out a cliché that, in your own mind, best describes your particular mask. Then move on to Step Three.

STEP THREE

Defining the Rules
of the Mask Self

THE PURPOSE OF THIS STEP

You'll define your Mask Self in its simplest terms, which are as rules, as in a game of chess. When you know these rules, you can quickly recognize both when and how they are influencing your choices and decisions. Your knowledge of these rules can be like red flags, alerting you to take a closer look at whether you are following your bliss or limiting yourself to the perceptions of your Mask Self.

BACKGROUND OF THE BENEFITS

Most of the behaviors that we associate with our Mask Selves can be broken down into a few simple rules. However, when you first start thinking about the Mask Self in these terms, you may feel resistance. This resistance will come directly from your Mask Self, trying to convince you that rules don't apply here. It may argue that rules are for suckers. They destroy spontaneity, and they restrict and limit what we can do. Your Mask Self may even try to convince you that it is the epitome of how it is to function without rules—always responsive, flexible, able to see the truth in any situation. However, in this step you will begin to see that it is the rules of your Mask Self that actually prevent you from responding directly to the present. You will see how the Mask Self is the source of rigidity and that it is quite bound up with the rules. Your knowledge of the rules can liberate you from these hidden rigidities and distortions associated with your Essential Wound and maintained by your Mask Self.

As sad as it may sometimes seem, we perhaps never completely free ourselves from our Mask Selves or the bitterness of our Essential Wounds. Some people say that these contain some of our most important spiritual lessons in life. And some argue that without them, we would go through life completely vulnerable, completely without psychological defenses or individualized contributions to make. Our knowledge of our own limited perceptions provides us with understanding and compassion for others, and lets us see that we are worthy even though imperfect.

If we can't be completely free of our Mask Selves, we can nevertheless learn to distinguish between the Mask Self and Inner Self and make our choices accordingly. We can choose to be open and vulnerable, following our bliss. Or we can choose to be guarded and closed, following the lessons we have incorporated in the Mask Self. Certainly there are times in our lives when both can be useful.

THE INSTRUCTIONS

In Step Two, you identified situations when your Mask Self was influencing your life. Go back to the material you discovered there. Record as much of this material as you can, embellishing with details and giving your Mask Self a name. (See the following section, "An Example," if you wish to see how this might look on paper.)

Now, in your journal, list as many rules as you can find that apply to your Mask Self. There are some simple tips that can be very useful for doing this.

Begin with the statement "When I am getting a high negative reading, I know I am seeing the world through my Mask Self. I then feel, think, and do the following." (Take a look at the following "Mask Self Rules Chart" and fill in the blanks, describing your experience as accurately as possible.)

MASK SELF RULES CHART

1. I feel: _____

_____

2. I think: _____

_____

3. I say: _____

_____

4. I do: _____

_____

5. I fantasize: _____

_____

As you begin, you may be tempted to make elaborate notes, explaining each rule and how it applies. If you start with an elaborate story, as Kris did, be sure to go back and simplify your work so that you have no more than one or two short sentences describing each rule. The shorter and more succinct the rule, the easier it is to remember and apply it in your daily life.

AN EXAMPLE

In Step Two we told you the story of Kris and James, whose relationship was being threatened by Kris's Mask Self, which she named "Mother's Little Helper." When Kris was asked to describe how she felt when she was wearing her Mask Self, she told the following story:

> As I was growing up, I always thought there was something wrong with me. I wasn't good enough to do what my brothers did, which was to spend time with my father, who liked to go hunting, fishing, to sports events, things like that. I didn't like all of these things, but I liked some of them. But the point was that I just wanted my dad to pay some attention to me.
>
> I always got treated like a "second-class citizen" in the family, with the boys and my father being first. My brothers, and even my dad sometimes, teased me, and my younger brother used to get me down and tickle me until I almost couldn't breathe. I hated that. It scared me half to death.
>
> I'd get real angry and run away to my friend's house next door. But when I thought about how angry I felt toward my brothers and my father, I just felt worse. I thought what I felt was just proof that I really was a second-class citizen in the family, because first-class citizens like my father and brothers never felt angry at each other. When they teased each other, they just took it as good fun, which is what they were always telling me.
>
> The only time I felt good about myself was when I helped my mom. I felt safe with her, that I was in the right place because she appreciated what I did for her and we sympathized with each other about how the others treated us.
>
> Lots of times I feel like a doormat, that I am here only to have people use me.

From this story, Kris filled out the "Mask Self Rules Chart" as follows:

MASK SELF RULES CHART FOR "MOTHER'S LITTLE HELPER"

1. I feel: There is something wrong with me. I am not good enough to do what my brothers do, which is spending time with Dad.
2. I think: I am a "second-class citizen." My brothers and my father come first.
3. I say: I say nothing because nothing second-class citizens have to say is of any value.
4. I do: I help Mom. She appreciates what I do for her, and we can sympathize with each other about how the others treat us.
5. I fantasize: The only purpose of my life is to let others use me in whatever ways they wish.

When she looked at the problems she was having in her relationship with James, Kris found the following:

She saw that even though no one was telling her that she was a second-class citizen, she was acting as if she were one, and she bitterly resented this. What she had not previously seen was that this was a key rule of her Mask Self. She perceived James as being far superior to her. Toward herself she was feeling extremely self-critical and self-effacing.

Unlike Kris's brothers and father, James did not see her as a second-class citizen, but sometimes he tried to tease her out of being depressed or discouraged. Whenever he did this, she saw what he was doing only through the eyes of her Mask Self. She interpreted his teasing as being exactly like her brothers' teasings when she was a child.

As soon as she saw her reactions as reflections of the

rules of her Mask Self, she began to see that she was imposing onto the relationship perceptions of herself as a second-class citizen. She and James discussed her Mask Self rules, and he was able to see why his teasing, though well-intentioned, could trigger the confusion and resentment associated with his wife's Mask Self. He made the decision to be careful about his teasing. Likewise, she made the decision to be careful to remind herself that James definitely did not look upon her as a second-class citizen.

By examining her relationship with James in terms of the Mask Self rules, Kris discovered a very interesting thing. In the beginning, taking care of James had felt familiar to her because it allowed her to follow the rules of the Mask Self, which she knew very well indeed. She could continue to be Mother's Little Helper, just as she had done as a child. But after she stripped away the mask and began to follow the guidance of her Inner Self, she discovered a whole new way of relating to James. She began to see things about him that she had never seen before. She said of this experience, "It's like finding I have fallen in love with an entirely different person than I thought I had, and he's really great!"

As she stripped away the mask, she had allowed her own Inner Self to come through. Her full, rich, loving Inner Self completely connected with James, allowing both of them to see the other in new ways. They began to see each other not as characters playing out the roles written by their Mask Selves, but as separate and whole beings, thinking and feeling and acting out the truths of their own hearts and minds.

There is an important point we'd like to make here. It is that in situations like Kris and James's, it is absolutely critical to see that the "homemaking chores" and "taking care of James" are not, of themselves, what causes Kris to feel uncomfortable and resentful. These tasks only trigger those uncomfortable perceptions within herself that she learned as a child. The tasks themselves aggravate our Essential Wounds, but they do so only as long as those wounds stay hidden behind the Mask Self. The moment Kris began healing her wounds, she could see that she had choices. She discovered, for example, that there were things she really enjoyed about being a homemaker. When she felt she was doing it out of love—rather than being compelled by her Mask Self—she thoroughly enjoyed doing things that made James happy.

AN ASSIGNMENT

As you go through the day, pay attention to your Homing Device. Whenever you get a negative reading, stand back and take a look at the Mask Self rules you may be applying to the situation that you are finding uncomfortable. Recognize that your Mask Self is most compelling when you are feeling threatened, anxious, or depressed. At these times, be alerted to the fact that you may be seeing the world through the limited vision of your Mask Self. You may be projecting that vision out onto the world in terms of one or more of the rules you've defined here.

The alternative to following the rules of your Mask Self, of course, is to follow your bliss. But when you are feeling distressed, that may seem like a remote possibility. Sometimes the only way to do this is to go deep into our own Lens of Perception and begin healing the Essential Wounds that are at the root of the Mask Self. Go on to Step Four if you wish to begin this process.

STEP FOUR

Healing Your Essential Wounds

THE PURPOSE OF THIS STEP

In this step, we go behind the Mask Self to look at those early experiences that we call the Essential Wounds. The goal here is to begin healing those early wounds so that we can lift the Mask Self and increase our trust in our own inner guidance.

BACKGROUND OF THE BENEFITS

We have already discussed how our lives are determined to a great extent by our own perceptions. We described our Lens of Perception as being something like an inner world to which we constantly turn for ideas and models. We usually use these ideas and models without thinking, giving them the power to guide us in our activities in the external world.

We also said that many of these ideas and models were formed early in our lives, long before we had the knowledge or experience to look at them critically. Thus, old perceptions that may have served us as children may now be hindering us, preventing us from either our own inner guidance or the knowledge we have gained since those early years.

Lucky for all of us that our perceptions aren't static! We aren't just stuck with whatever perceptions we absorbed in our youth.

As long as we have the willingness to do so, we can create new perceptions and change old ones. Yet how many times have you heard people whose lives are filled with one melodramatic crisis after another say, "Well, that's just the way I am." They go around acting as if there's just nothing to be done. They may argue: "I got dealt a bad hand, and that's just the way it goes. Some people are born lucky and some are born unlucky. I guess I'm just one of the unlucky ones."

The remedy for negative or unproductive perceptions is to recognize that you can rally up your greatest inner resources and start creating the inner perceptions you really want. You can create a Lens of Perception that will guide you along your true path, allowing you to follow your bliss undaunted by self-doubts or the cruel self-censorship of your Mask Self. The alternative is to passively submit to the perceptions we learned as children.

As ambitious as changing our inner perceptions might appear to be, the task really is not as big as one might think. It helps to know that we are not talking about changing the whole thing. As a general rule, much more is right with our perceptions than is wrong. The areas that we might change are really minuscule compared to the healthy and positive base that is available to every one of us.

We know that within us we already have what we have called the "Homing Device," which helps us identify what is on the path and what is not on the path for us. That Homing Device need not be changed. It is ready to work as it is, and it will serve us well once we learn how to make sense of the messages it sends to us.

All our changes will take place in our Mask Self, the source of all perceptions of nonsupport, fear, and lack of love. So how do we do this? How do we work with the Mask Self to create a more positive inner world, freeing us to follow our bliss? We do it by looking very closely and carefully at our "perceptual parents," that is, the mental images that we hold of our parents within our Lens of Perception.

At one time or another, most of us have said to ourselves, "If I had only had a parent who was more understanding!" or "If I had only had a father who would step in and tell my mother to stop screaming at us!" or "If I had only had a father who would stand up for me and encourage me when I did things on my own!" In the following pages, we'll show you how you can create just the parents you've always wanted. We'll also discuss how your creation of these new perceptual parents can help you follow your bliss.

Most of our Essential Wounds are based on our perceptions that our parents failed to support and nurture our unique inner realities. Notice that we say "our perceptions." Whether or not these perceptions are 100 percent accurate doesn't matter in the least for our purposes here. What matters is the perception itself, since it is the perception, even more than the "truth," that creates our inner realities.

You might ask, "How can it possibly be that a perception that I would deliberately create right now could change the perceptions I learned from my parents long ago?" The answer is that we do not change those early perceptions per se; but we can enrich and expand those inner realities that serve as our models for our decisions and actions in the external world. We can add more positive and supportive qualities to our inner, perceptual parents. Our goal in making these changes is always to increase our trust in our own inner guidance, giving us the insight and courage to follow our bliss.

The scientific basis for this process comes from the work of Drs. Elmer and Alyce Green, carried out in the 1960s and 1970s. They conducted an extensive research program on biofeedback, funded by the Menninger Foundation and several other prestigious scientific organizations. The Greens' was one of the most ambitious studies concerning the effects of the mind on the body ever subjected to the rigors of scientific scrutiny. One of the Greens' key discoveries was that the unconscious mind, which is home base of our inner reality, doesn't distinguish between real and imagined experiences. Within the unconscious, fact and fiction are one.

Consider what this means to us in terms of enriching our overall perceptions of life. First and foremost, it suggests that we might be able to deliberately broaden and enrich our inner worlds with new material that would give us a more positive and constructive view of our human potentials. We can, like painters expanding the range of colors and shapes on their canvases, expand the worlds in our own Lens of Perception.

For our present purposes, you might find it useful to think of your unconscious mind as a giant canvas, upon which you can paint any number of wonderful new pictures. Or, if you have a penchant for gardening, you might consider your unconscious mind as being like a huge plot of very rich soil, where you can plant anything you wish. Or, if you have an interest in interior design, you might see your unconscious mind as a huge mansion, with many rooms that you can organize, rearrange, and even populate with interesting people. Whatever your profession or hobby, there will be a metaphor that will work for you. You will be creating a new inner landscape, and when it is done, you will begin to see it mirrored in the external world.

THE INSTRUCTIONS

Start by going back to your gift, as we discussed it in Chapter 4. Refer back to notes you made in your journal on this subject. You'll recall that our full recognition of our gifts is often obscured by the Mask Self, which, in turn, is the product of the Essential Wound.

For a moment, focus your attention on at least one aspect of your gift, as you identified it in Chapter 4. Ask yourself, "How would I like this gift to be recognized? Would I like to be praised? Would I like recognition in the form of having one or both of my parents come to me for advice or help in this area? Would I like a more tangible reward?"

In your journal, list personal qualities of your own that you would like your perceptual parents to acknowledge and support. Describe these qualities in the most flattering ways you can.

EXAMPLE

Mary, the woman interested in animals whom we introduced in Chapter 6 wrote:

"I have an extraordinary ability to understand and communicate with animals. I have a real genius for making friends with them and creating a trusting atmosphere where they can feel safe and secure. I am convinced that my calling is in helping animals."

If you have more diverse gifts, such as those Susan described in Chapter 4, you may want to list each one separately.

EXAMPLE

1. I am a gifted observer. I can stand outside a situation and look in, seeing the whole dynamic at work. I have the ability to see process unfolding and to reflect it back to people.

2. I have wonderful planning abilities. After observing the situation for a while, I match a step-by-step plan to the process I've observed.

3. My body is my world. I have the ability to observe it from within, and to translate the observations I make here to problems another person may be having with his or her body."

Spend sufficient time with your list so that you really become convinced that you have these abilities and that you are very proud of them. When you're satisfied with how you feel, convinced that you are giving yourself as much credit for them as you would like to receive from other people, go on to do the following:

Imagine one or both of your parents in front of you. Remind yourself, before you go on, that the parents you are putting there are your own perceptual parents. You have total control of them. Even though your physical parents in real life might not have listened to you, you are completely free to create perceptual parents who will. Even though your physical parents in real life might not have gone along with what you are now asking them to do, your perceptual parents will. They are your creation, and you are free to give them every personal quality you always wished your real parents would have.

Now let your imagination go wild. Imagine your parents fully acknowledging the personal qualities or gifts that you have already listed. Describe exactly how you would like this positive acknowledgment to take place.

EXAMPLE

"I imagine that I am sitting in the living room with my mother and father. I say to them, 'I have something very important to tell you.' They stop everything they are doing to give me their full attention. Then I go on to tell them all about my gifts. I imagine them listening with great interest. I imagine them asking all the right questions, ones that reveal to me that they are interested in me and that they love listening to me tell them about my gifts."

If you find that you have too much resistance to having your real parents support you in this way, create surrogate parents who will show a sincere interest in you. When we were children most of us had fantasies that this friend's mother, or that friend's uncle, or another friend's big sister, would have been a much better parent than our own was. If this was the case for you, you might like to have these surrogates stand in and take part in this exercise.

If, as you examine your Essential Wounds, you discover that one of your parents was abusive toward you, discounted you, or frightened you, you may want to have that parent change, reinforced by the other parent.

An interesting thing begins to happen as you re-create your parents in these ways. Through the creation of these new inner world players, we gain new insights and new strengths. We find ourselves demanding respect and recognition in the external world which we previously didn't even know how to ask for. Those supportive qualities that we've instilled in our new inner parents become our own—just as occurs when we have real parents who are supportive.

To thoroughly ground these inner parents in your life, call upon them for assistance whenever you need them.

FIVE STEPS FOR RE-CREATING
YOUR PERCEPTUAL PARENTS

1. Identify your gift.
2. Decide how you would like your gift to be acknowledged by your perceptual parents or surrogate parents.
3. Imagine your parents giving you their undivided attention as you describe your own gifts in the most flattering way possible.
4. Imagine your parents fully acknowledging your gifts. (If one parent or the other intrudes with a nonsupportive comment, imagine the other parent stopping the intruding parent and insisting that he or she be supportive.)
5. Anchor your new perceptual parents by applying the new qualities you have given them in real life—giving you support when you are confronted with a challenge in the real world.

AN EXAMPLE

Dorothy's mother was very jealous of her when she was in her teens because Dorothy was a beautiful girl, something her mother always wanted to be. Her mother would look for qualities to pick on in Dorothy, such as, "You are just as empty-headed as every beautiful blonde." Although Dorothy was in fact a very intelligent woman, she grew up believing her mother's undermining comments and became extremely self-conscious whenever she found herself around educated people.

Dorothy had a definite gift for writing, but she was so intimidated by her mother's assessment of her intelligence that she simply wouldn't pursue it. When it came time to do this exercise, she imagined her mother putting her down. But then she had her father butt in and say, "Now,

Sharon (Dorothy's mother's name), you know that what you're saying just isn't true. Dorothy is quite intelligent and has a real gift for writing."

After Dorothy's father disciplined her mother in this way, Dorothy was able to imagine her mother and father together, listening to Dorothy as she described her gifts. Dorothy was eventually able to create perceptual parents who supported her in every way.

A few months after she had done this, Dorothy decided to enroll in a creative writing class she had always wanted to take at her local community college. The day Dorothy went to sign up, she felt extremely nervous. She began to experience the same self-doubt that had nagged her for years. This time she recognized this self-doubt as her mother's voice, telling her that she was just another "dumb blonde with no mind of her own." When this happened, she imagined her father stepping in, telling her mother that she was wrong and that Dorothy was not a dumb blonde but a very talented young woman. Dorothy signed up for the class, and near the end of the semester, had a poem she'd written accepted for the college literary magazine.

One of the side benefits of this exercise occurred when Dorothy decided to show her mother the magazine in which her poem was published. Dorothy expected her mother to find some way to put down her achievement, perhaps by belittling her accomplishment. Much to her surprise, her mother did just the opposite. She was ecstatic about the publication of the poem, and she ordered several copies of the magazine to send to relatives!

AN ASSIGNMENT

It is helpful to keep ongoing journal entries of any work you do with your newly created perceptual parents. Give yourself the assignment of going over this work several times, embellishing details each time you do. The richer the details, the more effective your new perceptions will be. For example, you might write more and more detailed physical descriptions of your perceptual parents: such things as what they are wearing, where they are sitting, the tones of their voices, and their facial expressions. It is important to move your perceptions out of the abstract into the physical, that is, give them identities with as many sensory cues as possible: how they look, what they say and how they say it, whether they are active or passive, and so forth.

Each time you use these new perceptions to support your gift and your own inner direction, you gain strength and confidence, literally moving you forward to trust your own inner guidance, giving yourself a clear path to follow your bliss. Keep records of your progress in your journals by telling short anecdotes of how your *new parents are helping you.*

Up to now, most of what we have discussed has concerned ways of identifying and healing those parts of us that get in the way of our trusting our inner guidance and following our bliss. At this juncture we'll be changing our emphasis, exploring the positive messages that provide us with guidelines for following our bliss.

STEP FIVE

Discovering Peak
Experience Patterns

THE PURPOSE OF THIS STEP

You'll dissect the patterns of your own peak experience, revealing the conditions you require for following your bliss in your relationships, your work, and the more routine activities of your daily life.

BACKGROUND OF THE BENEFITS

Peak experience are moments in our lives when we are fully actualizing our inner resources. Although these experiences usually take place within brief time spans, they epitomize what it is to follow our bliss.

The key characteristics of peak experiences are that during them, we are highly inner-directed, at the same time that we are perhaps as open and responsive to the world around us as we can possibly be. Each peak experience has a magic all its own, and this magic reveals much to us about following our bliss. Even though it can seem very elusive at times, it is possible to explore just what this magic is and how we can make use of it in following our bliss.

One of the very interesting things about peak experiences is that they have highly individualized patterns. That is, like good stories, each one has a beginning, middle, and end. And also like good stories, the way each of these cycles unfolds is as individualized as the "author" creating them. Every peak experience a person has follows a pattern that is uniquely characteristic for him or her.

The patterns that our peak experiences reveal to us give us many important clues about ourselves. They are like red lines indicating the preferred roads on a road map, showing us the best route for following our bliss. Each of these patterns is unique, which is why one person cannot prescribe a particular path for another.

So how do we find our own patterns? How do we uncover these all-important clues to the inner mysteries that guide us along our true paths? The following instructions will answer this.

THE INSTRUCTIONS

Back in Chapter 2 we introduced the concept of peak experience, and you did an experiential exercise for getting in touch with three or four of these experiences in your own life. At this time, go back to your previous records of this work. Take time to read the brief journal entries you made there to refresh your memory about the experiences you recorded.

If you did not find three or four peak experiences to work with at that time, or if you want to go into that same material in greater depth, read the next three italicized paragraphs. If you are already satisfied that you have three or four good peak experiences to work with, skip the next three italicized paragraphs and go on to the paragraph immediately following them.

Sometimes when people are first asked to recall peak experiences in their lives, they become intimidated. They feel "I have never done anything very outstanding in my life, so I could not possibly have had a peak experience." However, we all have peak experiences, almost without exception. Many times, these can seem very private and unimportant to other people, and perhaps they are.

To find peak experiences in your life, use your own feelings, rather than your own intellectual judgments about how important these experiences might be in other people's eyes. The best tool for doing this, of course, is your Homing Device. Go back and explore experiences in your life that felt very good to you. Look for ones that rate high on the positive side of the Readout scale of your Homing Device.

Recall moments in your past that were particularly pleasurable for you. Happy moments. Moments of ecstasy. Moments when you felt wonderfully pleased with yourself, deeply satisfied with whatever you were doing. You might think of moments when you were in love. Or when you were suddenly moved, deep within, by a piece of music, a book, a creative activity, a moment spent in nature, an athletic event, or a time when you were just "playing around" with no particular purpose in mind.

After recalling three or four peak experiences, choose the one that most interests you, or that you feel had the biggest impact on you. While focusing on this incident, tell the story of what happened, writing it down in your journal. (Some people prefer to use a tape recorder.)

Here are some key questions to think about prior to your recording these stories:

1. How did you get involved in this experience in the first place?

2. If other people participated, how would you describe the relationships you had with them?

3. Were there challenges (either imagined or real) involved? A handicap to overcome? A threat? Perfect calm? Any other influences that may have motivated you?

4. Was there any kind of preparation involved? Or was the lack of preparation itself a positive factor?

5. How committed, excited, interested, were you in the beginning? The middle? The end?

6. How important was the outcome in your mind?

7. What organization or lack of it was involved?

8. Was there a *turning point* for you, a moment when your level of involvement, energy, or interest suddenly changed and you started to put more of yourself into it?

9. Was there a reward that was important to you?

10. How did the experience end?

After recording your stories in as much detail as you feel is necessary to adequately describe your experiences, start looking for common patterns in all of them. Begin by working with the story that you found most impactful for you. Here's how:

Look at how you first got involved in the experience. This might involve something you read, heard about from another person, or imagined. Here are two examples of how people have reported this beginning cycle of their patterns:

I don't know where my first spark of interest begins, but usually it has to do with something I've been thinking about for a long time. One day I discover I've just jumped in with both feet and am trying something that I've been considering for weeks, or maybe even years.

Or:

My peak experiences have all started with watching one of my friends doing something that they seem to enjoy a lot. I get drawn into what they're doing and want to be a part of it. I'm a bit timid at first, but I get into it pretty quickly.

Always look for what is real for you on a deep, emotional level, rather than for what seems reasonable. Remember, what you're trying to discover and embrace in this work is your own inner reality. That reality, whether reasonable or not, whether like anyone else's or not, is what provides you with the cues for following your bliss.

When you are satisfied that you have identified the peak experience pattern for your first story, go on to the remaining stories and look for those same elements in them. There may be some parts that appear in some stories but not in others. Consider each element carefully, then make a list of *only those elements that appear in at least three stories*. Discard any elements that do not appear in the majority of your peak experiences.

If you wish to test any item in your pattern, get it clearly in mind—thinking about it, feeling it, etc.—and then subject it to a Readout with your Homing Device. Every item on your pattern should get a high, positive reading, in the range of a Positive 5 or better. If it fails to meet this test, discard it or consider refining the way you've written it.

Most people spend considerable time refining their peak experience patterns. Remember, the goal here is to get the pattern down in as simple, direct, and impactful a way as you can. What you should finally end up with is a list similar to the one in the example below, entitled "Karen's Peak Experience Pattern."

AN EXAMPLE

Karen teaches music in the public schools. She is married, has a seven-year-old daughter, is in her midthirties, and is very athletic. In her spare time she is a marathon runner who competes in amateur runs throughout the state. Many of her peak experiences have occurred during runs, but she has also had them while spending time with her family on vacation, while listening to music, and while doing more routine things in her daily life.

Karen reported that all her peak experiences started when "something grabbed my attention." She noted that this usually involved running, music, or something to do with her family. This was followed by a period of solitude. During this first cycle, she is sometimes accused by her friends and family of being "withdrawn" or even "depressed." She admitted that she always feels "detached" during these times but that she does not feel depressed, sad, or alone. In searching for descriptions of what she felt, she used words such as "meditation," "rumination," and "daydreaming," though she was not aware of doing any of these deliberately at the time.

The middle cycle of Karen's peak experiences was what she called the "research and practice" cycle, though she used the term very loosely. For example, if a marathon competition was involved, she would do everything she could to find out where the run would take place and what the course looked like. She would call at least three other people who had previously made the same run and pump them for information. Then she would train in similar terrain while mentally rehearsing the various hazards and challenges about which she'd learned.

For Karen, the final cycle had four distinct parts: The first part was a period of *enforced concentration*, during which she would allow no interruptions or distractions. The second part was a period of *psyching herself up*, during which she literally carried on an inner dialogue in which she told herself that she was fully prepared, that she had within her everything she needed to be wildly successful.

Karen called the third part of the final cycle "*letting go.*" It was in this period of time that she took action on everything that had gone before. To describe how this felt to her, she said: "It's like the instructions for everything I need to do are stored on this tape recording inside me, and I know it's going to come out right. I just *switch on* and let the tape go, and then it's as though all I have to do is follow what it says."

The fourth part of the final cycle was simply what she called "The Finish." The Finish came when she had completed what she had set out to do and had shared the outcome—either success or failure—with at least one person who was very close to her.

In every peak experience Karen could recall, she found this same pattern. Although she had never noticed it before, she now saw that it applied whether she was running a marathon, performing a piece of music, presenting a special lesson in the classroom, spending time with her family, or doing a project around the house. All peak experiences in her life, large or small, humble or ambitious, followed the same pattern.

For the peak experience pattern to be useful, we always suggest that it be broken down into its simplest elements. Here's how Karen's pattern looked after she simplified and refined it in this way:

KAREN'S PEAK EXPERIENCE PATTERN

1. **Beginning Cycle:** (This cycle has two parts for me.)
   (a) *Something Grabs My Attention:* I find myself attracted to an activity that involves running, music, or my family. I may hear about this activity from another person, read about it, or sometimes imagine it.
   (b) *Solitude:* I go into a period of solitude, a sort of ruminating period when I daydream about whatever has interested me.
2. **Middle Cycle:** I research the subject and begin practicing, preparing myself for what lies ahead. I work alone but may share what I'm finding with Mat (husband) or a friend.
3. **End Cycle:** (This cycle has four parts for me.)
   (a) *Enforced Concentration:* I create periods of time when I put all my attention into the thing I'm going to do. For periods of a half hour to an hour, I make sure that I am not interrupted for any reason.
   (b) *Psyching:* I talk to myself like a coach, telling myself I am great, that I'm going to go out there and succeed, that I'm fully prepared and everything about me is tuned in on what I'm about to do.
   (c) *Letting Go:* I take action. I picture having everything I need to know and do stored on this tape cassette inside me. I *switch on* and let the tape play, and then all I have to do is go with the instructions.
   (d) *The Finish:* When I complete the run, or whatever, I share the outcome and everything I'm feeling with someone close to me.

After she became acquainted with her Peak Experience Pattern, Karen began using it as a guideline in her life. In preparing for a run, she used it as a training plan, making certain that she completed each of the steps in her pattern. When preparing herself to present a special lesson to her classes, she again used it as a guideline. She used her knowledge of her pattern prior to working out problems with people at work and at home. And she even used an abbreviated version of her pattern in approaching routine chores in her life.

In each case, Karen found that her Peak Experience Pattern provided her with what she called "the musical score" for following her bliss. She explained that this was the musician's equivalent of a "road map."

AN ASSIGNMENT

Write down your Peak Experience Pattern on a card that you can carry around in your shirt pocket. From time to time in the days ahead, stop to take a look at how this pattern fits or doesn't fit an activity you are involved with at that moment. Especially take a look at those activities that you find pleasurable, or where you feel you are excelling. What you'll probably discover is that the pattern easily applies in these situations. By contrast, you will also discover that the pattern doesn't apply in those situations you find unpleasant, or where you feel you are not performing well.

You'll quickly begin to see that your Peak Experience Pattern shows up in every situation where you are—in one way or another—following your bliss.

STEP SIX

Cross-Referencing Your Peak Experience Pattern and Your Gift

THE PURPOSE OF THIS STEP

At the end of Chapter 4, you recorded what you felt was your gift. Here you'll take another look at your gift and incorporate it into your Peak Experience Pattern.

BACKGROUND OF THE BENEFITS

Our gifts, knacks, special talents, sensitivities, and abilities are key ingredients for following our bliss. Without them, we are not fully committing ourselves to the activity in which we're involved. Without our gifts, there is not that special spark that makes the activity truly worthwhile for us. However, when we are engaged at a level that incorporates our gifts, the *chemistry* changes, and we move into the realm of the peak experience.

204

Ideally, your Peak Experience Pattern will include clear guidelines showing how your gifts fit in and how you would make use of them.

THE INSTRUCTIONS

Turn to the journal entry where you recorded your Peak Experience Pattern. Mark that place and turn back to the list you made of your gifts from Chapter 4.

Now look carefully at your Peak Experience Pattern. Does it already reflect ways that you might use your gifts? If so, you need go no further. If it does not, look for ways to incorporate your gifts in the pattern. Revise your Peak Experience Pattern accordingly so that it reflects each and every item on your gift list.

AN EXAMPLE

In evaluating her gifts (Chapter 4), Karen had written the following:

1. I am talented in both music and athletics, doing well in these activities during most of my life. People appreciate and enjoy my musical abilities, and I think I've been an inspiration to other women, as well as my daughter, in my athletic achievements.

2. I have an ability to spend time alone and concentrate on any problem or on a subject that interests me until I begin to come up with ideas for making it work.

3. I have a high degree of self-sufficiency, or what most people call "highly motivated" or a "self-starter," yet I enjoy sharing those emotional times of success and defeat with other people who have helped me along with their support.

4. I have a knack for getting to the heart of something, for gathering information about it and organizing it in useful ways.

Take a look at this list and then refer to "Karen's Peak Experience Pattern" on p. 202. Notice how each of the four parts of her gift fits into her pattern. If you'll study it closely, you'll see that the Peak Experience Pattern has fully incorporated every personal gift she listed.

AN ASSIGNMENT

As you go through the normal events of your day, take a closer look at what you are doing. Note activities that you particularly enjoy, and see if you are expressing personal gifts there that you have not yet noted. If so, incorporate them into your Peak Experience Pattern.

Putting It All Together

THE PURPOSE OF THIS STEP

The best way to fully incorporate new knowledge in our consciousnesses is to apply what we've just learned to real situations, particularly ones that are affecting us right now. In this step, you'll use everything you've already worked with in Steps One through Six to create a clear mental picture of the conditions you require to follow your bliss in your work and your relationships.

BACKGROUND OF THE BENEFITS

To one degree or another, most of us are good at "adjusting" to a variety of conditions. At work we adjust to the requirements of our employers, and most of the time we put their needs before our own. We get up early in the morning and arrange our days to be on the job during certain hours. We take breaks at the allotted times throughout the day. We produce at certain levels. And we arrange vacations to accommodate company needs. "After all," a little voice within us says, "they're signing your paycheck."

Similarly, when we seek solutions to disagreements or emotional discomforts in our relationships, we often do so by *compromising*—a practice that usually ends up with no one getting exactly what they want. As one expert on conflict resolution put it, "Compromise is the fine art of negotiating an agreement which is equally unsatisfactory for all parties concerned."

Unless we're hermits, we cannot, of course, go through our lives without taking other people's needs into consideration. But there's a problem with meeting others' conditions without also giving a great deal of attention to our own. If we are primarily leading our lives according to other people's conditions, it is virtually guaranteed that we will not be giving our all. Because we'll not be working in a way that allows us to best access our personal resources and abilities, we will be producing at less than optimal levels in our jobs. And in our relationships we will be only half-heartedly involved with the other person. Though we don't necessarily intend it to work out that way, an important part of who we are simply is not engaged. The bottom line is that we are just *not* following our bliss.

When we're asked to describe our ideal work situations or relationships, most of us think in terms of specific vocations (engineer, manager, teacher, consultant, etc.) or in terms of physical descriptions (tall, blond, athletic type, etc.). We are generally much clearer about these choices than we are about the *quality of our relationships* in our work or with the people in our lives.

Certainly the choice of vocation and the physical description of a person are important parts of our choices, but these alone will not sustain us in the long run. We can get the job as a manager, and we can win the heart of the tall blonde, but unless rather specific conditions are met on a day-to-day basis, we will not risk the involvement of our Inner Selves. We will not be able to follow our bliss.

What, for example, will happen if the tall blonde turns out to be vain and domineering, while you are a person whose Peak Experience Pattern requires respect as an equal? The answer is that you will end up putting all your energy into trying to change each other, rather than relaxing into acceptance and love. And what will happen when you, a person whose pattern reveals a high regard for humanistic principles, lands that job as a manager only to discover that your employer has rigidly prescribed ways for dealing with every personnel problem? The answer is that you will feel resentful of that employer, and end up either trying to change the policies or subvert them in protest.

In our society, we are all too often taught to put the cart before the horse. We are taught to look outside ourselves to see what choices are being offered, then to adjust to whatever our choices require of us. But to follow our bliss, we must look inside ourselves first. Here we'll discover who we are, what we have to contribute, the kinds of things that delight us, how our very highest potential is best triggered or encouraged.

If we are to follow our bliss, automatic compromise or blind adjustment to others' conditions is the last thing in the world we want—for ourselves and for other people. Instead, we want to be as fully engaged in our work or relationships as humanly possible. And we want the people who we're involved with to be the same. This means three things:

1. It means looking for new ways to meet the conditions of our Peak Experience Patterns in our work and in our relationships.

2. It means knowing the kinds of things that "push our buttons," causing us to hide behind our Mask Selves, thus pulling us off our true paths so that we are not following our bliss.

3. It means knowing how to correct our course and get ourselves back on the path.

How do we make choices from the inside out, rather than the other way around? How can we identify what we can do to make our greatest contributions? How do we go about doing that in a way that will bring out our greatest personal resources and potentials? All these are achieved by creating a very clear mental picture, or impression, of what you require to follow your bliss, beginning with a simple process of cross-referencing your Peak Experience Pattern.

If you've done all six of the steps we've described in the workbook section, you will now have all the skills you require to accomplish all of the above. In the following instructions we explain how you can put them all together.

THE INSTRUCTIONS

The following instructions tell how to create a picture of your ideal work situation, or your ideal relationship, based on the needs of your Inner Self. The same instructions work equally well for work or relationship, but do just one at a time, starting with whichever one is most interesting or pressing to you at this time.

Get out your Peak Experience Pattern, as you defined it in Steps Five and Six. Study your entire pattern for a moment. Then go down through the list, item by item, asking yourself how each one of them will look when actually applied to your work or relationship. Transpose each item on the list from abstract principles to practical instructions that are descriptive and easy to follow. Here are some tips for doing this:

• Write each item on your list in the present tense, as if your ideal work situation or relationship were already a foregone conclusion. Write: "I *am working* with people who communicate well with one another," rather than: "I *will be working* with people, etc."

- Start each item on your list with the phrase "In my ideal work situation (or relationship) I am (or have)..."

AN EXAMPLE

The following sample shows you how Karen (whom you know from previous steps) did this for her work situation. You may wish to refer back to Karen's Peak Experience Pattern (Step Five) to compare how she adapted the original wording of her pattern to the following:

SAMPLE

(Adapted from "Karen's Peak Experience Pattern," Step Five)

1. In my ideal work situation, I am involved in at least one of my real loves. These are music, family, and athletics (preferably running, but not exclusively that).

2. I have a lot of variety in my work, and there is plenty of freedom to bring in my own ideas or projects.

3. I have time to mull over anything new that I want to bring to my work, and I feel at ease about this because I am sure my employers respect and trust me in this, never thinking that I am being lazy or not applying myself just because I'm not running around looking busy.

4. I spend some of my time researching, which I enjoy doing very much, though I don't want the whole job to consist of this.

5. I have periods of considerable challenge, such as giving public concerts and competing (usually against my own standards).

6. There is plenty of opportunity to have quiet time to myself so that I can prepare in solitude, without interruptions, during periods when I am starting new projects or getting ready for concerts, etc.

7. I have at least one close friend and coworker with whom I share my experiences.

As she reviewed the preceding list, Karen was quickly able to see that her present profession, which is teaching music at a high school, fits her pattern quite well. But what happens when a person's present job doesn't fit? Here's an example of how one person handled this problem:

Adjusting the Job to the Pattern

Keith was a manager for a large electronics company. One of the most important things he had learned about himself was that all his peak experiences had started when he was called upon to step in and solve a special problem or a crisis. At his present job, things generally went pretty well, and few real crises occurred. Although most people would have been quite happy to have a job with so few complications, Keith felt bored and unchallenged.

When this was revealed in the workshop he took from us, one participant quipped that Keith could create his own crisis now and then, thus meeting a key condition of his Peak Experience Pattern. However, Keith himself came up with a better solution. He went to his employer and described the difficulty he was having. He pointed out that he had great skills as a mediator, and was extremely effective at resolving conflicts that arose in the workplace. A week after the workshop, we learned that the supervisor had promoted Keith to a position where his Peak Experience Pattern would be put to better use: as a troubleshooter in the factory where he worked.

The lesson here is that sometimes we can go to our employers and negotiate changes in our work assignments. After we know the conditions of our Peak Experience Patterns, we can easily identify how our present work matches up and we can ask for different responsibilities to help make better use of these patterns.

More often than not, we can meet the conditions of our

patterns not by changing jobs but by simply expanding our responsibilities or changing the ways we perform present ones. Here's another good example:

Expanding the Job Description

Deborah was the executive secretary for the CEO of a large wholesale clothier. She discovered that her peak experiences all involved a public performance. In high school and college she had taken drama classes and had been in several theater productions, which she thoroughly enjoyed. Although for a variety of reasons she did not want a career in theater, she did enjoy public presentations.

We asked her if she saw any opportunities in her life, either at her job or outside it, to stand up in front of an audience and make presentations. At first she said no. Then it suddenly occurred to her that her boss made several different kinds of public presentations each year, to the board of directors, to the sales staff, and so forth. He hated doing these presentations with a vengeance, and consequently was not very good at them.

Deborah made her boss an offer. She would help him put these presentations together in a more stimulating way, using visuals such as overhead slides and flip charts. She could directly assist him in this, and since she was attractive, witty, and had training in public speaking, she would be a welcome asset in delivering many parts of the reports. Her boss leapt at the opportunity to have her assist him.

With this plan, Deborah not only satisfied an important part of her own Peak Experience Pattern, her participation in these presentations took a great deal of pressure off her boss. And needless to say, the audiences to these "performances" were eternally grateful. Previously they had found them to be painfully boring. Now, thanks to Deborah, they found them to be inspired and even entertaining at times.

Adjusting Relationships to Patterns

A conflict in Karen's marriage offered the opportunity to see how the Peak Experience Pattern could help solve relationship problems. While transposing her original pattern to her relationship, Karen immediately came up against the source of a present conflict. It had to do with her need to be alone.

An important part of Karen's pattern was solitude and privacy. The trouble was that Karen, her husband, and their small child lived in a tiny two-bedroom apartment. When Karen wanted privacy and solitude, there was simply no place to find it. This led to arguments with her husband. He had no need for as much solitude as she required, and he was having a great deal of difficulty understanding why Karen needed it. He was really of the opinion that something was wrong with her.

When Karen saw what the problem was, she initiated the changes. She sat down with her husband and pointed out that, right or wrong, solitude and privacy were part of her pattern. From looking at a number of situations in her life, it was very clear to her that she dealt with pressure best and most effectively when she was able to have a certain amount of privacy and solitude to think things through.

Karen and her husband discussed different ways that she might get this, finally deciding that when she absolutely needed time for herself, she could tell her husband what she needed. He would then watch after their daughter while she went out for a short drive in the car. There was a park nearby, where Karen could rest and enjoy an uninterrupted period of time to work things out in her own head. Then she could go back home with renewed energy and enthusiasm. This arrangement worked out quite well, with her husband soon being able to see that their relationship went much smoother when Karen took the time for her solitude.

The following is how "Karen's Peak Experience Pattern" looked after she adapted it for her ideal relationship:

SAMPLE

(Adapted from "Karen's Peak Experience Pattern," Step Five)

1. Bill (her husband) and I share a number of interests, at the top of the list being music and family. Although he does not participate in athletics himself, he seems to enjoy coming to the meets where I run, which is great because he is always as excited as I am to talk about the run after I've completed it.

2. Bill and I like to bounce new ideas off each other about everything under the sun, so I feel that I have plenty of room in our relationship to express my ideas.

3. Although it was not always that way, I can now feel at ease about taking time to mull over any problems or ideas that I'm working on, and to have Bill respect my needs in this area.

4. Neither Bill nor I move quickly on things—we both like to look ahead and research or carefully consider all our options—and so we give each other a lot of support when it comes to processing questions or decisions that come up.

5. We both enjoy music, and partly because of this, Bill supports me completely when I take time to prepare for concerts at school or other special projects I'm involved in.

6. Although I have friends at school to talk things over with, I feel that Bill is my closest friend. I don't think there is anything we couldn't speak about with each other. He's a wonderful listener.

When the Mask Self Intrudes

Sometimes, regardless of how well our work or our relationships seem to match our Peak Experience Patterns, we still feel that we are doing *anything but* following our bliss. Something seems to be pulling us off our paths, and at least for the time being, we are certain that we are not following our bliss.

When this happens, it is time to take a look at the Mask Self. It is time to ask ourselves to identify what is triggering our doubts or fears, causing us to want to hide behind our masks, and causing us to look at the world through its eyes. At such times we usually find the negative influence within ourselves, rather than in the external world.

When you do have periods of time when you feel particularly negative about your work or relationship, go back to Step Three of this workbook section, "Defining the Rules of the Mask Self." Review the list you made in your journal describing the rules of your Mask Self. You might then wish to go on to Step Four to heal the Essential Wounds that are presently affecting your work or relationship.

AN ASSIGNMENT

More often than not, the key to following our bliss is simply knowing what we want and letting the world know what that is. We fail to get what we want from life not because the world doesn't offer the opportunity, but because we fail to ask. But asking is a special art in itself. Where following your bliss is concerned, asking begins within you. It begins with a clear mental image, a defined impression, a descriptive list or other expression of exactly what it is we want in our lives.

Just as the negative influences of the Mask Self cause us to find negativity in the external world, so our clear positive images of what we want from life cause us to find the opportunities for fulfillment both outside and inside us. In this respect, our Peak Experience Patterns are like beacons glowing through the darkness. It is a beacon that reveals the opportunities outside us, even as it lets the world know where we stand and how to find us.

In the weeks ahead, pay a great deal of attention to the patterns you've defined for your relationships and your work. Look for opportunities to apply what you've learned from these lists to seek out the ways you can more perfectly match the patterns with whatever you are doing. Let other people know you a little better by looking for appropriate openings when you can express or make use of your gifts and your conditions.

When we find the courage to trust the power of our Inner Selves, following our bliss is easy. And that courage starts within, by knowing and learning to trust our Peak Experience Patterns, and healing the Essential Wounds that prevent us from seeing that our gifts truly are worth giving.

AFTERWORD

A Note from the Authors

Coauthoring a book of this kind is perhaps one of the ultimate tests of a relationship. One of the main reasons is that writing is ordinarily a very solitary and introverted activity. For a while, within the landscape of the emerging book, the author can play God, master of his own paper world. But when you write with another person, your ego-salving game of playing God must be shared, and that's not always easy, even with a person you love with all your heart.

Besides learning to work together and love in that most private inner world of the book, working with an idea such as we present here forces you to take a closer look at your own life. It is like putting yourself under a microscope. As we thought about the ideas we discuss here, we couldn't help but become deeply introspective and cross-examine ourselves. We found ourselves asking, "Am I following my bliss in my work at this moment? Am I trusting my inner guidance in my relationship right now?"

Sometimes it was quite clear that we were not practicing

what we were preaching. There were times, both in writing the book and in our lives outside it, when we were doing *anything but*. At those moments we felt that if we were following our bliss, it certainly didn't feel like it. As with any project that extends over a long period of time, there were times when we found ourselves "efforting" far too much. Following your bliss, we thought, should be easy and fun. Instead, we sometimes seemed to be at the mercy of deadlines, cash flow, and the usual frustrations, self-doubts, and minor but aggravating trials of daily living. And, like anyone else, there were times when we felt that there were just too many demands being made on us and we didn't seem able to find the path where we felt that we were truly following our bliss.

In addition to the times when we felt we were at the mercy of the world around us, there were also times when we found ourselves trying, with great effort, to force the external world into our own preconceptions of the way things should be. We forgot some of our own best advice in this, that whenever we are tempted to "take on the world," to change what cannot be changed in an effort to find peace, we are definitely not following our bliss.

One of the most valuable lessons we learned in writing this book was that following our bliss is at one and the same time the easiest and most demanding thing any of us can do with our lives. On the one hand, there is the ease and deep self-satisfaction that comes with doing what you know you're best suited to do. When you follow that path, there is no doubt that at the end of the day you feel great about yourself, high on the fact that in following your inner guidance, you can make an important contribution while satisfying what on the surface seems like a very selfish need. On the other hand, following your bliss demands the most from you because it demands the very best that you have to give.

During the time that we were writing this book, there were many major changes in our lives, some of which were momentarily disruptive, though we can now say they were positive in the long run. One of our grown children, who we thought was out on her own forever, came back to live with us for a while longer. That certainly caused us to reevaluate our lives. Then, soon after this, we purchased our own home and faced the physical and emotional challenge of moving and getting used to a new place.

As we faced the more dramatic changes that life presented, we were reminded of yet another lesson: that the decision to follow our bliss offers no guaranteed twenty-four-hour-per-day protection from the many "disturbances" life offers. Nevertheless, when we are following our bliss, the disturbances along the way grow pale. It is a little like having the security of knowing that you're following the best map you can possibly get when you're taking a long trip across the country. You may make a wrong turn now and then. You may have engine trouble. You may find yourself forced to take overnight accommodations that are less than delightful. But these little sidetracks don't hurl you off center; you maintain the confidence that you are on the right path. In a short time, you'll arrive at the destination you dream of and you'll feel wonderful.

Working on the book kept us focused, kept us asking ourselves how following our bliss made a difference in the quality of our lives, moment by moment, day by day. For example, we found ourselves looking with new eyes at the usual pressures of running one's own business: checks late in arriving, taxes due, manuscripts lost in the mail, important phone calls not returned, clients canceling at the last moment, and so forth. These were certainly additional stresses in our lives, resulting in short periods of conflict and confusion that felt anything but blissful. But then the clouds of self-doubt, anxiety, and frustration cleared and we again found confirmation that, for the long term, we were following the right map. We were on the right track, both in the book and in the bigger picture of our lives away from the book.

If we learned nothing else about following our bliss at

this time, it was that it is very important to keep the *bigger picture* clearly in mind. Even though we may be following our bliss, and trusting our inner guidance, life doesn't suddenly turn into a flawless Utopia. There are still the normal problems of living that can cast shadows of doubt and fear; only in retrospect can we see that our resolution of these problems within the context of following our bliss not only cleared the air but also helped to broaden the pictures of our own life paths.

A TIME TO LOOK BACK

Writing this book has been a time for us to look back and to take a closer look at where we've been, at what our lives have taught us. We discovered, for example, that from the time we were very young, we had shared a belief in following our own inner guidance. Our parents would claim that we were "headstrong and stubborn children," for surely that must have been the impression we sometimes gave.

In comparing notes about why we'd led our lives that way, we agreed that it hadn't been a conscious decision, at least not when we were very young. It was more a matter of just never being able to imagine that there was any alternative. A lot of this had to do with the way we grew up. Both of us spent an important part of our early lives in rural areas—Susan high in the Sierras, where her parents owned a mountain resort, Hal in a very beautiful rural area of Michigan, surrounded by lakes and rivers and forests.

When we compared notes on our early lives, we both found that, growing up as we had, we were simply naive about many of the societal expectations and economic pressures of urban living. Until high school, we led relatively poetic lives, comfortable with our own inner worlds, turning to them, as often as not, for our own entertainment and amusement. Although we didn't have a name for it then, we were familiar with using our inner resources and following our inner guidance. Much of the time there really weren't any other sources of guidance. We learned to trust our inner guidance not because we had read somewhere that this was a good thing to do, but because in nature, where we spent so much of our time, that was the only place we could find anything resembling workable answers.

As we grew into young adulthood and moved to the cities, however, all that changed. We had to learn how to pay much more attention to the external world, to look, to listen, and to make decisions based upon the harsher realities of urban life. And for periods of time, the demands of the external world seemed to drown out the inner signals we'd come to depend upon in our early lives. It took a long time to integrate the lessons from our childhoods with the lessons of adulthood, and to finally return to that very early trust we had once had with our inner worlds. It took time to rediscover that what we see and hear and smell and feel is not just "out there," but that it is the result of an interaction between the external environment and what we bring to it from within.

BACK TO THE FUTURE OF THE SIXTIES

As young adults during that period of time, the 1960s certainly provided support for our beliefs. If those years gave us nothing else, it was the experience of being surrounded by extraordinary opportunities to explore the nature of our beings, to go inward and discover possibilities that had lain hidden and dormant within the human psyche for perhaps thousands of years.

Daily encounters with the transformative music of groups such as the Doors, the Jefferson Airplane, the Moody Blues, backed up by psychedelic light shows, self-expressive free-style dancing, love-ins, sit-ins, and the use of hallucinogens, we clearly saw only one thing—that *life was certainly not what it appeared to be.* We saw that life could be shaped and molded, that it was perhaps possible to create a world from the inside out, that there was a very real possibility that having the kind of world we all wanted truly could be a choice. We did not have to be victims of a world that we had innocently inherited.

That was where the bridges began to be built back into mainstream America, through the movements that addressed the universal problems of human beings the world over, such as health, interpersonal relations, and finding what we ourselves are all about. The bridges came in forms such as the holistic health movement, and the human potential movement, spearheaded by the Esalen Institute at Big Sur and other mirror images of it that sprouted up around the country. Realizing the power of our individual choices, we added the lessons history had taught us about collective bargaining and organized labor of the thirties and applied then to the causes of civil rights, ending the Vietnam War, and stopping the nuclear arms race. We had at least enough success in these to be convinced that it could work, that we didn't have to be bound forever to the decisions of those who presumed to be our leaders and authorities.

The sixties produced two important groups: One might be characterized as having learned the power of challenging the outer limits, of pushing outward, of freely playing with imagination, fantasy, and illusion to create new ways of perceiving the world, with new technologies and new styles in art, design, science, technology, and music. The other group might be characterized as having explored the inner world, discovering the power of the human consciousness to influence itself, the physical body, and to interact with a collective consciousness that embraced all of life.

As the sixties died, and those of us who had participated

in this great experiment moved toward middle age, we suddenly found ourselves back in mainstream America, worrying about job security, medical insurance, raising our families, buying cars and houses and television sets and computers, and wondering how in the world we were ever going to pay for our children's college educations. In the midst of it all, we couldn't ignore what we had learned in those intense, sensual, wonderfully creative years. How could we possibly make use of it all?

Had it all been just an interlude, a passing dream and an "escape from reality" that would have little to do with the rest of our lives? Had it all been a weekend visit to a carnival, whose bizarre world, created so convincingly under the big top and along the midways, had nothing at all to do with the world and couldn't be transplanted back home? Or was there something more important in all this, something that we could carry on into *everyday life*, something that could truly enhance the quality of life for ourselves and the generations to come?

In the sixties, while the Jack Kerouacs and Allen Ginsbergs and Ken Keseys and Tim Learys and the Beatles and the Grateful Dead, and so many others that there is no space to mention, were challenging sacred cows and pushing back the boundaries, there were also the Buckminster Fullers, the Joseph Campbells, the Abraham Maslows, and the Aldous Huxleys, who were calmly sitting back, reflecting, and consciously or unconsciously laying the foundations upon which we would eventually build the bridges that would allow us to link the historical past with the turbulent present and the yet-to-be-revealed future.

Probably every one of us who was a part of the sixties can now look back and identify with one group or another, breaking down walls and pushing limits, or going inward and wondering how we were ever going to build bridges into the future. If we had learned anything at all about self-reflection in the process, we had also come to respect our own inner worlds and to see that each one of us holds within us the power to create a not-so-private hell or a world of peace and harmony and love never before known here on earth.

THE DAWNING OF THE NEW AGE

And then came the "New Age," a new and powerful signal to begin building those bridges we'd known for a long time had to be built. As an extension of the sixties, the daring inventiveness of that earlier time has been replaced by a more sober, more reflective, more pragmatic, yet lighter and more spiritual base from which to work.

As we responded to this new influence, we began to see that the sixties had only barely masked the ethic of "rugged individualism," which had served us well during the pioneering period of our country but was now blinding us to a broader, richer vision. We had put an awful lot of emphasis on individual effort, as though we believed that a single person standing alone could accomplish it all. The New Age brought us a giant step beyond that, showing us that we all share a spiritual link, a place where we are all One. With this new perception comes the realization that we are never alone, and that our shared visions of peace and love and Oneness can ultimately accomplish more than all the armies in the world. For those of us who were so deeply involved in the sixties, the underlying ethics of the New Age offers the opportunity to apply much of what we learned then, but now with a vision that goes beyond the limits of our physical beings.

From our new perspective, we find skills from the ancient, intuition-based cultures of Egypt, the Far East, and the shamanic societies of the Americas. From them we are learning cooler, more disciplined ways of working with the power of human consciousness when it is stretched beyond the limits of those styles of thinking and feeling associated with our modern technological world.

In the process of living our lives with a quiet commitment to certain beliefs and experiences from the sixties,
we have become convinced that inner guidance can provide us with a sense of purpose and meaning beyond our
wildest dreams, if we only take the time to learn how to
listen to our Inner Selves.

THE CHALLENGE OF LOOKING INWARD

We would never claim that either one of us has mas-
tered the art of decoding all the messages from our Inner
Selves so that we can always follow our bliss. Rather, we
must confess to our process often being one of trial and
error. There continue to be periods when we feel that we
have surely chosen the wrong path, and that our choices
will certainly lead to disaster. Looking back to review how
we've done, we see many successes, but we have also
experienced many difficult challenges: divorce, the death
of loved ones, and the hopes, fears, joys, and sorrows of
helping to raise five children.

As parents, we sometimes look at our children and see
in their lives a reflection not only of our strengths and our
love and our selflessness, but also of our weaknesses and
our intolerance of others and our selfishness. If there are
lessons in parenthood, they surely must be found in learning forgiveness, and in accepting our own humanness and
the humanness of all others who share this planet with us.
And in a funny way, all these reconfirm the importance
of following our inner guidance.

Again and again we have been reminded that following
our inner guidance inevitably means confronting ourselves in ways that, admittedly, aren't always without
pain. When we make the decision to follow our bliss, we
take on a commitment and a risk. It is a commitment to
face our fears and self-deceptions so that we can look beyond them. It is a commitment to find our inner voice, to
follow the song and the special rhythms that make up the

unique "heartbeat" of our own lives. It is a commitment to stop blaming the external world for blocking our way. It is a commitment to start seeing the people and events that come into our lives as teaching us something about ourselves, mirroring back to us the illusions and perceptions of our inner worlds. And it is a commitment to take full responsibility for these illusions and perceptions in order to free ourselves to give the greatest gift any of us can ever give, ourselves.

In spite of it all, we were convinced that one can only go wrong by *not* following our bliss. Yet, as sure as we are of that, it doesn't ever completely free us of occasional self-doubt. That simply seems to go with the territory. There will always be questions: "Can I maintain the pace? Can I do what I must do to follow through with my choices? What if I misread my inner direction and find myself on a wrong path? What if I discover that, while I satisfy myself in following my inner guidance, the world finds no value in my quest, and I find myself neither supported nor loved in this solitary adventure? What if by following my bliss, I discover that my path leads me to a wilderness where I am isolated and alone?" The amazing thing is that the only thing one has to fear in making the choice to trust one's inner guidance is the loss of courage. As someone once said, "Tenacity is nine-tenths of success."

Now that the book is done, we can look back and say that in writing it, we were truly following our bliss. But we have to confess, there was more than a single time when we stopped to look at each other and ask, "What gives us the authority to write this? What are our credentials? Where's the proof that we have anything valuable to say on this subject?"

In mulling this question over one day with a friend, he suggested that we were asking the wrong questions. We were not, after all, wanting others to look upon us as "high priests." Unlike high priests, we had not learned our lessons from books or by studying the sacred laws, as priests did. Although we certainly weren't ignorant about such things, the real contribution we could make was found in the direct lessons of our life experiences.

"Like the shaman," our friend said, "your value to others isn't that you've lived exemplary lives, pure and without fault. With the shaman, almost the opposite is true. The shaman's healing power comes from the fact that he has died and come back, or that he has been crazy and is now sane, or that he has violated sacred laws and now reveres and teaches them. Or maybe it is that he has struggled with a life-threatening disease, and even with the disease still in his body, he is living a good life. Or it is that he was once selfish, alone, and without love, but is now filled with love that others can feel in his presence. These are the things that bring healing to those who are facing such challenges for the first time. They can look at the shaman and find hope, seeing that there is another way of looking at their own lives, that here before you is living proof that you can overcome the difficulties you face."

While we might prefer the analogy of being shamans rather than high priests, perhaps the real message in this is that for any of us, the lessons of our own lives—some rising out of joy and success, some from sorrow and failure—are the best we have to offer. Somewhere in the space between the limits of our own perceptions and our illusions, we discover a truth that can never be stated because there are no words to embrace it all. And we can come to this place any time that we are willing to clearly see, then accept, forgive, and love our own and each other's humanness.

In the final analysis, it is only this humanness that we have to give. It is the greatest gift we can offer. In our innocence we might judge it imperfect. But when we are on the path of following our bliss, we know that it is enough.

OTHER BOOKS BY THE AUTHORS

If you enjoyed reading *Follow Your Bliss*, you may also enjoy one or more of the following books:

Write From the Heart: Unleashing the Power of Your Creativity (With a special chapter on Getting Happily Published.) This is Hal's 25th book, this one presenting his revolutionary ideas on creativity and the role of writing in personal growth. Based on 30 years in publishing.

Zuni Fetishes: Using Native American Objects for Meditation, Reflection and Insight. This is a beautifully illustrated book on Native American spirituality and the use of animal carvings as "power figures." Learn how to use this system to boost your own creativity and explore inner resources. A divination system that has stimulated creativity for centuries. 50,000 in print!

Lens of Perception--The Roots of Creativity. Explores the workings of creativity and human knowing—the shamanic roots of wisdom. This underground classic is praised by leading authors such as Terence McKenna, Lynn Andrews, Shakti Gawain. Gabrielle Roth describes it as "full of fascinating insights into the mysteries of human perception."

Inner Guides--Audio Recording. In this tape Hal & Susan explore the subject of inner guides and spirit companions of the deep, creative consciousness; takes you through a guided meditation to meet your own guide. Brings together creativity and intuition.

Inner Guides, Visions & Dreams. Over a decade in print, this book tells you everything you need to know about spirit guides, dreams and even your daydreams. Has been a favorite with writers. Explore the richest resources of your deep creative consciousness.

0-595-31659-X